GRACE ALONE

Grace Alone

LUTHERAN IN THE 21ST CENTURY

Rev. Katherine Rohloff

Rohloff Publishing

First Printing, 2020

Contents

Dedication   ix
Confirmation Covenant   xi

Five Solas: Lutheran Basics   1

Small Catechism: Ten Commandments   **9**

Why Have Commandments?   11
Commandments About God   17
Commandments About Relationships   23
Commandments About Community   29

Small Catechism: Apostles' Creed   **35**

Creator Almighty   37
Jesus Christ   43
Holy Spirit   49

Small Catechism: Lord's Prayer — 55

Teach Us to Pray — 57

Addressing God — 63

Our Needs — 69

Small Catechism: Sacraments — 75

Communion: What God Does — 77

Communion: What We Do — 83

Baptism: What God Does — 89

Baptism: What We Do — 95

Church History — 101

Early Church to the Great Schism — 103

Reformation — 109

Lutherans & WWII — 115

Slavery and the Bible — 121

ELCA History — 127

Faith Structure — 133

ELCA Structure & Ministries — 135

Career Ministry — 141

Other Lutheran Denominations — 147

Other Christian Denominations — 153

Other Religions   159

Church Calendar   **165**

Season of Pentecost Holidays   167

Seasons Related to Christmas   175

Seasons Related to Easter   179

Faith Life   **185**

Priesthood of All Believers   187

Spiritual Disciplines   193

Stewardship   199

Worship Whys   205

Special Services   211

Special Topics   **217**

Lutherans & The Bible   219

The End of All Things   225

Spiritual Self Defense   231

Oppression in the Bible   237

Science & Faith   243

Appendix: Bible Study Guides   249
Appendix: How to Use This Book   281
Acknowledgments   287

Works Cited   289
About The Author   291

This is dedicated to some of my favorite people: my students.

For inspiration, I sincerely thank all my former Confirmation students at St. Martin's in Cross Plains, WI and at Peace Lutheran in Ryan, IA.

For their feedback, patience, and enthusiasm, I especially thank my Confirmation students who were the first to use this program at Scandian Grove Lutheran Church in Norseland, MN: Cole, Nathen, Summer, Ruby, Seth, Sydney, Sara, and Tyler.

Confirmation Covenant

At my baptism, my family and sponsors promised that we would live among God's faithful people; that they would bring me to the word of God and the holy supper, teach me the Lord's Prayer, the Creed, and the Ten Commandments, and place in my hands the holy scriptures. They promised to nurture me in faith and prayer, so that I may learn to trust God, proclaim Christ through word and deed, care for others and the world God made, and work for justice and peace. They have promised to help me grow in Christian faith and life.

The Confirmation ceremony is a public Affirmation of Baptism, which means to make those promises for myself: to live among God's faithful people, to hear the word of God and share in the Lord's supper, to proclaim the good news of God in Christ through word and deed, to serve all people, following the example of Jesus, and to strive for justice and peace throughout the earth. Going through the process of Confirmation is preparation for those promises.

Therefore, during the Confirmation process, I promise to:
support my fellow students and pray for them,
do my best to live in harmony with all God's children,
worship as often as I'm able to, to hear the word of God and receive Communion,

proclaim God's love for all people with my words and my actions,

help others with humility and generosity,

and work for justice and peace wherever I can.

And in all this I ask God to help and guide me.

_____

Student's Signature/Date

As a representative of the people of this congregation, who in turn represent Christians throughout the world, I promise to support this Confirmand in their life in Christ through prayer and any help I can give them. I will teach them to the best of my ability, help them to grow in faith and love, and treat them with respect as a fellow child of God. As a baptized Christian, I will fulfill my own baptismal promises by living with them in harmony, sharing with them the word of God and the holy supper, proclaiming God's love for them in my words and my actions, helping them with humility and generosity, and working with them for justice and peace wherever we can. And in all this I ask God to help and guide me.

_____

Pastor's Signature/Date

Five Solas: Lutheran Basics

Reading: Psalm 46

Hymn: Dear Christians One And All Rejoice ELW 594

Sola Scriptura (2 Timothy 3:14-17)

These five ideas began as a way for the Lutherans to explain how they were different from the Catholics, but today they summarize what makes Lutherans unique among the many Christian denominations. The first three are the oldest: *sola scriptura, sola fide,* and *sola gratia. Sola scriptura* translates to "by scripture alone." It stands for the concept that only scripture, rather than tradition or anything else, is the most accurate and important source we have for doctrine and church practice. It is also sometimes phrased by saying the Bible is the "source and norm" ("norm" meaning measure or baseline) for faith and Christian life. *Sola scriptura* does not mean that we don't pay attention to tradition, or to the wisdom of Christians present and past. The world has changed extensively in the past two thousand years, and the Bible does not directly address some modern-day concerns or ethical dilemmas. But everything we do; our faith, ethics, and even worship liturgy, are grounded in scripture.

You may be familiar with Christian groups who proclaim they believe in "Biblical inerrancy," or "Biblical literalism." *Sola scriptura* is rather different than these, though some Lutherans do hold to those ideas as well. "Biblical inerrancy" states simply that nothing in the Bible is wrong. "Biblical literalism" states that everything in the Bible happened, literally, as stated, rather than understanding some stories as metaphors or parables. *Sola scriptura* does not require either of these, but it does keep the Bible a powerful authority in the church and Christian life.

1. Like all of the *solae, sola scriptura* has basis in scripture. Take a look at the verses from 2 Timothy above. Do you think they are a valid scriptural basis for *sola scriptura*? Can you think of any other Bible verses or stories that talk about scripture?

Sola Fide (Romans 3-4)

Sola fide translates to "by faith alone," and stands for the concept that it is through faith alone, rather than through good works or actions, that we are saved. This isn't to say that Christians shouldn't or don't do good works - many Lutherans have said over the years that a person's faith becomes obvious to others through works. Helping others, being kind and charitable, generous and honest: these are how any Christian would share the love of God with all people, as scripture commands us to do over and over. But our doing these things is not why God extends grace to us - instead it's by our faith.

This also isn't to say that Christians can do anything they want, or sin as much as they want, because their faith means they're saved. Sin is often made obvious through broken relationship or through objectification of people (thinking of people as objects, or as a means to an end). God's love is steadfast and unrelenting, and we have been commanded to love one another as God loved us. Sin is not a proof of lack of faith, either- we are all sinners, and fall short of the glory of God, even the best Christians.

Finally, this is also often misunderstood by essentially turning faith into a work. Faith isn't something we earn, or a merit badge we get once and then don't have to be concerned with anymore. Instead, faith is a gift of God through the Holy Spirit, which grows in us through our experience of the sacraments and hearing the Gospel read and preached. Growing the faith of people around the world is the mission and goal of the church - not just the Lutheran church, but the Christian church.

1. "Faith comes by hearing" (scripture, worship, hymns) is from Romans 10:17, and has become a popular Lutheran proverb. How do you think a person who is Deaf might say this? What are some other ways to share this idea?

Sola Gratia (Ephesians 2:8-9)

Sola gratia, or "by grace alone" expands on *sola fide*. It is by God's gift to us of grace, given freely, that we are saved. Again, not through our own actions or by anything we have or have not done. God's grace is not something that can be earned by saying a specific prayer or by never breaking a set of particular rules. God's gift of salvation through the death and resurrection of Jesus Christ is not so bound by humanity's rules or customs as to be powerless outside of them. This is a reason why the Lutheran church will baptize infants instead of only practicing "believer's baptism" of those who have publicly announced their faith. It's not our actions that cause God to grant grace, the choice is entirely God's.

In our society, we tend to doubt the worth of what comes to us freely. If we've paid a high cost for a piece of clothing or a gadget, we'll look after it carefully, but free trinkets we treat more carelessly. The cost of this grace was high, but we did not pay it - it was paid for with Christ's death and resurrection. We must treat the grace we've been granted with the respect due to that high cost. Dietrich Bonhoeffer illustrates how we treat grace as cheap, and what costly grace leads to, in his book *Cost of Discipleship*:

Cheap Grace	Costly Grace
preaching forgiveness without repentance	calls to discipleship
baptism without the discipline of community	calls us to follow Jesus Christ
Lord's Supper without confession of sin	costs people their (expected) lives
absolution without personal confession	causes people to live in Christ
grace that doesn't lead to discipleship	acknowledges & condemns sin
grace that doesn't acknowledge the cross	justifies (makes right with God) the sinner

"Above all, grace is costly, because it was costly to God, because it costs God the life of God's Son—'you were bought with a price'—and because nothing can be cheap to us which is costly to God."

1. Bonhoeffer gives a list of illustrations of what treating God's grace as either cheap or costly might lead us to do. Can you think of another example of either?

Solo Christo (Colossians 1:15-20)

Solo Christo translates to "through Christ alone" is one of the two *Solae* developed later on. The Reformers developed the idea of *solo Christo* in order to explain their differences on certain matters with the Catholic church, and the essential idea of it is that it is through Christ's death and resurrection alone, that we are saved, not through anything else. The Catholic church today would not disagree with this, and has said so in the *Joint Declaration on the Doctrine of Justification*, a document written with the Lutheran church to declare our agreement on related matters. However, the Reformers felt that certain practices of the Catholic church weakened the *perception* of this truth.

These three practices are the concept of purgatory, the veneration of saints, and the role of a priest as mediator between God and the faithful. (All three of these are rather complicated to explain fully and have nuances that require some study to fully comprehend, so the discussion of them here is *extremely* simplified. Further questions are best directed to a Catholic priest.)

- The Catholic doctrine of purgatory, a process by which God completely purifies repentant sinners so they may enter heaven, allows for living Christians to assist with prayers and good works.
  - The Reformers felt that this weakened the doctrine of *solo Christo* in two ways: by placing another layer, purgatory, between faithful Christians and God; and by stating that people's works could have effect on a person's state of salvation.

- In the Catholic practice of veneration of saints, the souls of honored Christians of days gone by are asked to pray for specific causes to God, in addition to a person's own prayer.
  - The Reformers, while valuing the lessons these admirable Christians can teach us, saw this mediation as unnecessary. We are saved through Christ; no other mediator is needed.
- The Catholic priest stands *in persona Christi*, as the physical presence of Christ.
  - This is why a Lutheran pastor absolving sins after Confession, will declare them forgiven in the 3rd person (God forgives you) and a priest will use the 1st person (I forgive you). The Reformers saw this in a very similar way to the veneration of saints.

1. Has someone ever misunderstood what you think or believe because of something you did, or perhaps you misunderstood someone else? When do our actions show others what we believe?

Soli Deo Gloria (1 Corinthians 10:23-31)

Finally, we come to *soli Deo gloria*, or "glory to God alone." This states that everything that a Christian does, is to be done for the glory of God, in celebration and recognition of the grace that has been extended to us. We do this not out of fear of punishment, but out of gratitude for the gift that has been extended to us in the death and resurrection of Jesus Christ. We also do not do good works for our own glory, or for what praise or rewards we may receive for doing them, but instead as a response to the love which God has already shown us.

Martin Luther encouraged this in many of his sermons and books by discussing ways that ordinary Christians could live their lives for the glory of God. He had conversations with his barber about how to pray and spoke at some length about farmers stewarding God's creation in farming. "The Christian shoemaker does his duty not by putting little crosses on the shoes, but by making good shoes," (presumably to better serve one's neighbor, who needs good shoes) is a quote often attributed to Luther. While we don't actually have record of him saying this, it does illustrate his emphasis on how all Christians can give glory to God in their daily lives through being honest and faithful.

1. Ask an adult you know who has a paid job, a bit about what they do. Then explain this idea to them and ask how they glorify God at their work. Then ask someone who doesn't have a paid job (a fellow student, a homemaker, or someone who's retired) how they live their life to glorify God.

This week I will pray for:

Small Catechism: Ten Commandments

Why Have Commandments?

Reading: Exodus 19:1-8

Hymn: Come Thou Fount of Every Blessing ELW 807

Who Needs Rules?

The 10 Commandments appear twice in the Bible, first in Exodus 20 when God first gives them to Moses to give to the Israelites, and again in Deuteronomy 5, when God repeats them for the next generation. There are a few small differences between the two passages, and while everyone agrees that there are 10 Commandments, there are several disagreements about how they should be numbered. The Jewish people numbered them one way, the Catholic Church changed it slightly, and many Protestant churches use a third numbering system. Lutherans use similar numbering to the Catholic Church.

Why do we follow the 10 Commandments? After all, we are saved by God's grace, not by our works, so what's the point of following the rules? We've discovered over the years that the 10 Commandments work well as a short way of describing how to live a loving and faithful life that builds up the people of God's creation, rather than tearing them down. They're not big or flashy, and they're easy to remember. But like learning the rules for the game of chess, they are easy to learn but harder to follow. They have deep and life-changing implications for how we treat one another. Following the 10 Commandments is a spiritual practice, something we can do to deepen our relationship with God.

Aren't there other Commandments too? Absolutely! Jesus, when asked what the greatest commandment is, said in Matthew 22:37-39, "'You shall love the Lord your God with all your heart, and with all your soul, and with all your mind.' This is the greatest and first commandment. And a second is like it: 'You shall love your neighbor as yourself.'" These are what the 10 Commandments add up to. Jesus also tells us during the Last Supper in John 13, his final commandment to us, to love one another as he has loved us. If you look in the Hebrew Scriptures, you'll also find the Holiness Code, which is a system of over 600 rules about who was worthy of entering certain parts of the Temple in Jerusalem.

1. You've probably received useful life-advice from family or friends. If you phrased one piece of advice as a commandment anyone could follow, what would it say?

Theology of the Cross

Martin Luther, in his many books besides the Small Catechism, contrasts *theology of glory*, with the *theology of the cross*. *Theology of glory* would say that we earn our way into God's love by doing good works, following the rules, and being "good people." It further says that if we do these things, a good, wealthy, and happy life will follow, because God wants those who follow the rules to be happy and will make sure it happens. This idea about how God works puts more emphasis on what we do than on what God does. It also easily leads to lots of very nasty implications: that some people are more holy or more loved by God than others; that respectability is more important than caring for others; that tragedy is a punishment; or that first impressions can tell us God's opinion of a person. This tells us that, if we see someone in trouble, our first instinct should be that it must somehow be their own fault. If this sounds familiar, it's similar to what some of America's pop culture claims Christianity is.

In contrast, *theology of the cross* says that everything we need to know about God, we learn from the cross: from Jesus' crucifixion. If we look at everything that God has done through the cross, from the beginning of creation until now, we see that grace was always the plan. God's law was given to us as a gift. It curbs our worst impulses, it shows us who we really are (because we need the rules in the first place), and it guides us. It also shows us we will never be perfect; whatever good we try to do, there still might be unintended consequences. God's law shows us that we will always need God's grace. As Luther said in his *Heidelberg Disputation,* "The law says, 'Do this,' and it is never done. Grace says, 'believe in this' and everything is already done." This says that, if we see someone in trouble, God's unrelenting love will overflow through us so we can help them. If this sounds familiar, it may remind you of some stories you've read in the Bible. This is what we embrace as Lutherans.

Basically, the difference is between appearance and substance. *Theology of glory* values appearances: if we appear to do and say the right things, then God will be with us and keep us from difficulties. It leads us to focus on bettering ourselves instead of helping others. *Theology of the cross* values substance: that God has always loved us and stays with us even in our most difficult times, because God understands suffering and has been there. It leads us to help others out of compassion and humility, because we understand that we are completely equal to each other in the eyes of God.

1. Are there some rules in your life that have more to do with appearance over substance? Do you think they're helpful, or can they hurt people who are already having trouble?

God on the Commandments

In the conclusion to the 10 Commandments section of the Small Catechism, Luther quotes Deuteronomy 5:9-10: "...for I the Lord your God am a jealous God, punishing children for the iniquity of parents, to the third and fourth generation of those who reject me, but showing steadfast love to the thousandth generation of those who love me and keep my commandments." That sounds terrifying! Why would God, who loves us, say something like that? But if we look into history, we know that breaking the Commandments can echo through the years. Violence leads to more violence. Even in one family, having a vividly remembered story of one family member who broke a commandment, can lead to their grandchildren and great-grandchildren making life decisions based, in part, on something that happened decades before. Our actions do have consequences, which can reach much further than we expect.

It is possible to appear to break a commandment by accident, but that isn't the same as doing so on purpose. For example, a witness to a traffic incident may not remember something correctly, even though they believe they do. When asking a crowd to describe a car that was present less than 20 minutes before, it's common to get several very different descriptions. As long as each person is doing their best to tell the truth, that's not breaking a commandment. Being wrong is not the same as perjury.

Ultimately, breaking the commandments on purpose is evidence of a broken relationship with God, and that's what sin is. When we do that, we are trying to push ourselves further away from the life that God would have us live, and further away from God. Often that broken relationship with God is reflected in broken relationships with others, and that can be a helpful guide. None of us can keep all of the commandments perfectly. But having them as a guide for living helps us to work towards a better life and future. And if we reach a point when we're not sure how to follow the Commandments correctly, we can go back to Jesus' final commandment, to love one another as he first loved us.

1. Pick a commandment where it's easy to see how breaking it could lead to a broken relationship with other people. How do you think that would injure a person's relationship with God?

This week I will pray for:

Commandments About God

Reading: 1 John 4:7-16

Hymn: Great is Thy Faithfulness ELW 733

No Other Gods

We read in Exodus 20 that the commandments were given to Moses on Mount Sinai by God, after God had led Moses and the Israelites out of slavery in Egypt, as they made their way to Israel. Given that background, the 1st Commandment makes a lot of sense: "I am the Lord your God, who brought you out of Egypt, you shall have no other gods before me." It also makes sense that Moses was horrified and embarrassed when he returned down the mountain to his people, only to find that they had created a golden calf and were worshiping it. In his anger, Moses broke the stone tablets he'd written the 10 Commandments on and had to return to the mountaintop for God to share them a second time. To no one's surprise, the commandment spells out that *idols* (false gods) and idol worship are not allowed.

Most of us aren't going to create a statue and begin worshiping it. What would breaking the 1st Commandment look like for us? There are a lot of ways we do this, but three ways stand out as the most common and obvious. First, we tend to put other people on a pedestal and imagine that they are perfect. In our hearts, we may long to be that person, or to be with them, beyond everything else. The problem with worshiping a person, is that they are not, ever, perfect. None of us are. While crushes and youthful infatuation are stages which many people go through, that is not a model for a healthy relationship. Part of a mature friendship or romantic relationship is recognizing one another's flaws.

The second way we put something ahead of God in our lives is addiction. Often addiction isn't something chosen on purpose, studies show there are genetic and environmental factors in how addiction works. Yet it is still putting one thing, an imperfect thing, at the center of your life, where God should be. When God is at the center of our lives, we are drawn to generosity, compassion, justice, and mercy. When an addiction is at the center of our lives, we are drawn to selfishness, envy, heartlessness, and cruelty.

Third is the most common of all addictions, which is money. We fool ourselves into believing that if we just have enough money, all our problems will go away. While there are certainly a lot of problems that money can help, it is still not something we can fully put our trust in. A health crisis, a job loss, or identity theft might all make very fast changes to a person's financial stability. Also, when we focus entirely on money, we tend to become more selfish and stop working for justice for others.

1. What's the difference between enjoying something, and worshiping (or being addicted to) it?

Wrongful Use of the Name
In the "Addressing God" lesson we read about the first phrase of the Lord's Prayer, "Our Father, hallowed be your name." To hal-

low a name is to treat it as holy. But the 2nd Commandment has a slightly different spin, now we're talking about using God's name wrongly. In older Bible translations, this was often called "taking the Lord's name in vain," which is a vivid way to put it. To take God's name in vain means to use it lightly, without purpose or meaning, as though it, or God, doesn't matter.

However, the full translation from ancient Hebrew is to say, "You shall not make wrongful use of the name of the Lord." Luther gives a list of examples of what not to do in the Small Catechism. We are not to use God's name to try to curse people or practice magic, as God is not a bully who is at our beck and call. We are not to use God's name in order to lie more convincingly, as though God would encourage us in the attempt. We can probably also come up with additional ways that using God's name would be wrong. We should not use God's name to be cruel to others, or to encourage or increase suffering in other's lives. We should not use God's name for our own ambition, to get ahead.

What does using God's name well look like? One way to think about this is to ask ourselves how our friends and family would feel about our using their names. They would probably be happy if we used their names while talking to them, or telling other people good things about them, right? Using a person's name to ask them for help is perfectly reasonable, or to say thank you. If you're talking about something you've learned, it's good to give credit to the person who taught you. And if you have something difficult to say to someone you love, even if you're not sure how they'll take it or if they'll thank you for it, they'll probably appreciate that you trusted them enough to be honest with them, and using their name then makes sense as well. So, we use God's name when we pray, evangelize, ask for God's help, give thanks, talk about what we've learned, or have difficult conversations with God.

1. Has your name ever been used in a way you didn't appreciate? How so?

Remember the Sabbath

And on the seventh day, God rested. The idea of a sabbath, or a day of rest, comes from the very beginning of Genesis. When Christianity began, we moved our day of rest from the seventh day, Saturday, to the day Christ rose from the dead, Sunday. Over the years this commandment has been understood in different ways. In the Bible we read of those who wanted Jesus to get into trouble and tried to enforce this rule on him in ways that would have hurt others (Luke 6:1-11 has two examples). But this Commandment is not a rule we follow from fear, but a gift we've been given from God. In Biblical times and for thousands of years afterwards, it made sure that even the poorest laborers had a day of rest once a week. This commandment isn't about forcing people to do nothing, but a gift of rest that we need!

We keep a day of rest because we need one. We can't work 7 days a week, 365 days a year, or our bodies break down. We don't just need to sleep at night, we need time to relax, time not taken up by work or chores or activities. That day doesn't necessarily have to be Sunday, as there are some jobs that have to have someone on call every day, such as emergency services. But as anyone who has worked a swing shift can tell you, having a full day off of work is very different than having a few extra hours here or there. Being away from work for a full day allows for a much deeper rest.

This day of rest also gives us the time to worship God. Ideally, worship is a daily activity, but on our busy days we can only devote a few moments here and there to asking God to be with us and guide us. On a day of rest, we can devote more time and concentration to worship, learning more about our faith, trying new spiritual practices, and nurturing the faith of others while being nurtured ourselves. This is why having a religious community is so vital to our faith lives. Christianity is by its nature community based. Our faith may be in our individual hearts, but faith always leads us towards others, over and over again. By discussing our faith with others, hearing ideas that are new to us, and discovering that the way that we are used to doing things is not the only way, our faith grows and becomes more vibrant. A faith community gives us encouragement, reality checks, lovingkindness, and guidance.

1. When have you received a reality check or helpful advice from another person? What might have happened if you hadn't received it?

This week I will pray for:

Commandments About Relationships

Reading: Mark 10:2-12

Hymn: Christ Is Alive! Let Christians Sing ELW 389

Honor Your Parents

How do we honor our parents in the modern world? Biblical examples aren't always very helpful: Abraham and Isaac, Lot and his daughters, and even Mary and Jesus had a few issues. And when we admit how complicated the real world can get, the question gets more complex: between biological parents, foster parents, adoptive parents, legal guardians, godparents, and more, who exactly does this commandment apply to? What about emancipated teenagers, or those with abuse in their family?

Luther says throughout the Small Catechism that our respect and love for God should lead us to relationships with others that are characterized by respect, love, and support, just as God loves and supports us. That's not just true for parents, but our relationships with all people. But our relationship with our parents - whether they are our parents biologically, legally, or by choice - is different than many of our other relationships because they are in a position of authority. Luther groups them in with others in authority over us - like our teachers, or the government - so this commandment applies to all relationships of authority. Relationships that involve authority are a little different than relationships between equals, because there are expectations and a necessary level of trust, because of that authority.

But sometimes those expectations and that trust are broken. How do we follow this commandment when the people in authority over us are dishonorable people? What does this commandment mean when we have parents, teachers, or other authority figures who are abusing those under their power, or misusing their authority to hurt others, or for their own gain? In those cases, we ask ourselves: what do respect, love, and support really mean? If we truly respect the position of authority, don't we want the job carried out in the best way possible? If we truly love a person, don't we want them to cause as little harm to others as possible? If we truly support our community, don't we want to keep all the members of our community safe? This commandment may be short, but that doesn't mean it's simple.

1. What are some stories from history or the Bible of people challenging authority figures in ways that follow this commandment? Are these stories of people you admire? Why?

No Murder

Some older translations from the original Hebrew make this commandment "You shall not kill," but a more precise translation is "You shall not murder." What's the difference? A person might be killed accidentally - in a car crash, for example - or a soldier might be killed defending their country. Murder, on the other hand, is the deliberate killing of a specific person, and is such an obvious sin that legal systems around the world have outlawed it. Many legal systems also allow that some circumstances change how severe the crime is, such as the murderer not being in their right mind and not realizing what they've done. A common controversy related to this commandment is the death penalty: does a nation have the right to execute criminals? In 1991, the ELCA published a Social Statement against the death penalty, citing statistics that show it has not made communities safer, and that it has been inflicted on the innocent.

Just as Jesus sometimes expanded on instructions from the Hebrew Scriptures (as you'll see in the passage from Mark for this lesson), Luther also expands this commandment to be about more than deliberate murder. He says that our respect and love for God will lead us not only to not murder others, but also to not harm them or cause them to fear, and to help and support them as we can. This brings this commandment more into the world of our everyday lives. When we look at others and ask ourselves: how can we keep them from harm? How can we keep them from fear? How can we help and support them? This is when the full meaning of the fifth commandment becomes clear.

What can this look like in our lives? We see harm and fear all too often: injustice, cruelty, bullying, terrorism, bigotry and more. This commandment calls us to act when we discover these in the world. Again, the love and support we receive from God call us to love and support others. Elie Wiesel, author of the Night trilogy on the Holocaust, said, "The opposite of love is not hate, it's indifference." Hate takes energy and effort; indifference takes neither and is a much more subtle, and common, danger. When we believe that another's suffering is not our business, we break the fifth commandment.

1. When have you seen someone indifferent to another's suffering? How did it make you feel?

No Adultery

Adultery isn't a word we use often: it means a married person having sex with someone other than their spouse. To commit adultery is to break the vow of faithfulness made in trust when getting married. Since a marriage is built on those vows made before God, this breaks the relationship between the married couple, and is another example of sin being broken relationship between people, and between a person and God. God's love and support of us calls us to love and support others, including our spouse.

So what does that love and support look like in a romantic relationship? First, let's separate love from possessiveness. Loving another person does not mean that you own them, or that they owe you anything, or that you can treat them with less respect than you'd treat anyone else. To love someone means respecting them: their choices, boundaries, and rights. Without that respect there can't be real trust. Being in a romantic relationship with someone doesn't mean you get to veto their friendships or family relationships, or you have to know every tiny detail of their life: both of these show a lack of trust.

One way we show that respect in a romantic relationship is to respect the importance of consent. As a romantic relationship progresses, making sure that your partner consents (not begrudgingly but enthusiastically!) to new steps or changes in the relationship is a very basic way of showing respect. In a marriage, for example, this includes consent about sexual activity, as a way to respect your spouse's choices and feelings. In all romantic relationships, consent involves respecting a person's private thoughts, documents, photos, and information - which means not sharing them without their consent. Ignoring consent, no matter the depth or length of a romantic relationship, is a sign of abuse.

Your worth as a person is not determined by your romantic life - you remain a beloved, baptized child of God no matter how your romantic life works out. Some people take several tries to find their life partner, some never find theirs, some never wanted one to begin with. Some people have lots of people who are attracted to them, some have fewer. None of that makes a person any more or less worthy of God's love, or a community's respect. Sometimes a romantic relationship ends, due to the decision of one or both people involved, and at that point the goal is to continue treating one another with the love and support that God has first given you, without vengeance, gossip, or malice.

1. In the 1940s & 1950s, "going steady" (dating just one person) was reserved for older high school students and adults and was a prelude to getting engaged. How has dating changed since?

This week I will pray for:

Commandments About Community

Reading: Luke 18:18-27

Hymn: Blest Be the Tie That Binds ELW 656

No Stealing

We keep learning that a commandment might sound simple, but have a lengthy ripple effect, and this one is no different. "Okay," we say to ourselves, "I won't steal, there we go." But stealing isn't just taking someone's dessert off their plate when they aren't paying attention, or "forgetting" to give back the change after someone gives you money to buy something for them. One of the types of stealing you might be familiar with is plagiarism: the stealing of ideas. Schools spend hours teaching how to cite sources and properly document bibliographies, to avoid breaking this commandment. Laying claim to an idea that isn't yours is just as much stealing, as laying claim to money or property that isn't yours.

But stealing goes further than that. What about a store that publishes false advertising, saying that a product has qualities people appreciate, when it doesn't? The money they make from that lie is another form of stealing. In the real estate market, this can get even more complicated, if a seller doesn't disclose a problem with a house or building. That lie can lead not only to a crooked business deal but might also endanger the new owners. An employee who goofs off during their shift instead of doing their job, is effectively stealing from their employer. "Tipped employees," like restaurant wait staff, aren't necessarily required to be paid minimum wage, on the assumption that their tips will take them over minimum wage. If their tips don't make up the difference, their employer is required to, but not all employers do, which means they are stealing from their staff. There are many ways that a lie - or information held back - can lead to stealing from another person or group.

Instead of stealing, whether directly or through "shoddy merchandise or crooked deals" as the Small Catechism puts it, Luther says we are to help our neighbors to keep and improve what they already have. If our neighbor has a medical problem and can't do manual labor for a time, we can mow their lawn or shovel their snow. If our neighbor is going out of town for a while, we can keep an eye on their place for them and take in the mail, so it isn't obvious they're away. If a farming family has a medical emergency, neighboring families will often step up to help with chores to get them through the emergency. There are lots of ways we can help our neighbors like this.

1. Are employers who don't allow their hourly employees to take the rest and meal breaks that the law requires, stealing from their employees?

No False Witness

This commandment is often understood as saying, "you shall not lie." This usually leads us into conversations about so-called "little white lies," or more bizarre conversations about things like whether it's right to lie to a blood-covered murderer about where someone is. These conversations might be interesting, but they miss the point of the original commandment: You shall not bear false witness against your neighbor. In a narrow sense, it's about the crime of *perjury*: lying in court while under oath. Civilizations around the world have had this law since the idea of courts have existed. In order for a court of law to dispense true justice, the trial must be based on the truth, rather than lies, opinions, or stereotypes. Most people are quick to agree that perjury should be a crime, for good reason.

But the commandments always have larger applications, as Luther points out in his explanation of this one. Since this commandment is about perjury rather than lying, the focus is not on lying **to** a person, but lying **about** them. Lying to a person breaks our relationship with them but lying about a person can do so much more harm, possibly breaking their relationships with many other people. This is why Luther, in his explanation of this commandment, says that we are called to not spread rumors or destroy the reputations of others by lying about them. If we don't know whether a rumor is true, spreading it might mean we are spreading a lie. This could destroy a person's relationship with their entire community, not just a few people, and many people have had their lives destroyed that way.

Instead, as we share the love God first shared with us, we are called to defend and speak well of each other. Not just for our friends and loved ones, but for all our neighbors and God's beloved children. Imagine a community where this was the usual type of behavior: wouldn't you want to live there? Luther also invites us to understand each other's actions in the "best possible light." We don't always know why someone does something, but we can avoid jumping to the worst possible conclusions before we know the truth. When someone shares a rumor, we can point out why rumors are a bad idea and ask for proof. Don't forget that the word "possible" is in there: we're not supposed to ignore evil or criminal actions, but if we don't know the truth yet, we can hope for the best.

1. How long has it been since you jumped to an unpleasant conclusion about someone, perhaps because of their behavior or appearance?

No Coveting Possessions or Relationships

The last two commandments instruct us not to *covet*, or be envious, of what possessions or relationships other people have. Envy is a powerful emotion, but not a constructive one. Think about it: if you want something, you can try to work for it. But if you are envious of something your friend already has, it's probably going to sour your friendship. Envy of possessions is one thing, but envy of relationships can be even more toxic. If you're envious of their loving relationship with their parents, or their supportive group of friends you don't share, it's not just going to sour that one friendship, is it? It could also make your relationships with their parents or your own parents, or their other friends or your own friends, more painful and difficult.

Envy can be an easy emotion to get stuck in, even addictive, and it can encourage hurtful decision-making. Envy gets us focused on who has what we want, rather than how we can get it ourselves, or even whether it really matters to us at all. We might spend two months focused on our envy over someone's new gadget, instead of two weeks of doing odd jobs to afford one for ourselves, or one week of odd jobs before realizing we don't want it after all. Instead of working to better our own relationships or seek out new ones, envy of another person's relationship might make sabotaging theirs look like a good idea. In the Small Catechism, Luther reminds us that God's love calls us to never try to steal or trick people out of what they have or the people in their life.

Instead, we are called as Christians to love and support our neighbors so that they can keep and maintain their property and relationships. So, at baptisms, confirmations, and weddings, everyone gathered promises to pray for and support the folks at the center of the celebration. These aren't empty promises either. When we enter a business relationship with someone, God doesn't call us to get every penny we can out of them, but to treat them with fairness and honesty.

1. We don't always realize we're envious right away. When we do realize we are, how can we turn that emotion from being destructive to constructive, and keep it from hurting our relationships?

This week I will pray for:

Small Catechism: Apostles' Creed

Creator Almighty

Reading: Genesis 1-2

Hymn: Of The Father's Love Begotten ELW 295

The Three Creeds

Why do we have creeds? A creed is a statement of faith, which explains the basics of the beliefs of a religion. Christianity is not the only religion with the idea of creeds. Islam has one, and some say that Judaism's creed is Deuteronomy 6:4. A simple, concise creed can be an easy way to sum up the basics of belief for students, and for those unfamiliar with a religion. Some Christian groups, while acknowledging that they accept the truth of the Christian creeds, avoid using them and focus entirely on each person being able to explain their faith in their own words. Certainly, creeds have their limits, and being able to describe the faith in one's own words is vital, but we still find them helpful.

One of the most important topics that the Christian creeds address is the nature of the Trinity. Christians are *monotheists*, worshipping only one God, and proclaim that God exists in three persons: Father Almighty, Jesus Christ, and Holy Spirit. Also called the Three-in-One and One-in-Three, the Trinity can be a complicated idea to explain to someone who didn't grow up with it. The "Shield of the Trinity" seen on the next page, is another traditional way of explaining the Trinity, for more visual learners. It shows that while the persons of the Trinity are all separate, they are still one as God. The church has had many disagreements about the nature and workings of the Trinity, and the creeds carefully avoid many common heresies on the subject, which have troubling implications about who God is and who we are to God, such as *Arianism*, below.

Lutherans accept and teach three creeds: the Apostles' Creed, the Nicene Creed, and the Athanasian Creed. The Apostles' Creed is probably the oldest, but we don't know precisely when it was written or by whom. It seems to have grown and been added to over the earliest years of the church. As the

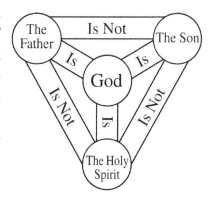

church grew, people had more questions about how Christianity worked, and a more complete creed was needed, so the Nicene Creed was adopted at the First Council of Nicaea in 325 CE. The Nicene Creed explains that both Jesus and the Holy Spirit are persons of the Trinity, one with God, and that Jesus is both human and divine. The Athanasian Creed is much longer and was written a few hundred years later, specifically to rebuke the heresy of *Arianism*, which claims that Jesus was created by and is inferior to God. Anyone can write a statement of faith for themselves, but these three carefully worded creeds have been accepted by the Lutheran church as useful for teaching.

1. If you wrote a creed, what's the most important thing about God you'd want in it?

The Father Almighty

Two persons of the Trinity, Jesus Christ and the Holy Spirit, are simple to name. The other person of the Trinity has many names: God the Father, Almighty God, or God the Creator. It can be difficult to tell the difference between referring to this person of the Trinity, and the entire Trinity, sometimes. One of the most common ways to distinguish this is to use the term "Father." The Bible frequently refers to God as our parent. It can be a fitting metaphor, since God is the reason we exist, and also takes on several roles in our lives that parents commonly do, such as providing for and protecting us.

We also use words like "Almighty" and "Awesome" to describe God. These help us to remember that God is all powerful and all knowing, beyond our comprehension. Nothing we can know or imagine is beyond the power or love of God. We cannot do anything to put ourselves beyond God's reach. Some ask, "Can God make a rock so big God can't lift it?" Questions like this, show how little we really understand of what God's power means. We could ask, are questions like these puzzles to God?

Of course, while the language used for this person in the Bible is often, though not only, masculine, God the Creator is not actually human, and therefore does not conform to our ideas of gender. Jesus was human, and male, but that does not speak to the nature of the rest of the Trinity. In Biblical Israel, women were not seen as being equal to men, and so God was usually referred to as male, but there are instances where God is described with feminine characteristics. Both men and women are "made in the image of God" in Genesis. Quite often God is described as a mother to God's people, perhaps most famously in Isaiah 66:13: "As a mother comforts her child, so I will comfort you...."

1. If a person has a troubled history with their father, they might want to use a different word for God. Think about what God is like. Do you have relatives, or others, you can see God in?

Creator of Heaven & Earth

Everything that exists comes from God, from the smallest atom to the largest galaxy, from the most irritating mosquito to the most beautiful stars in the sky. All of the objects we manufacture come from materials created by God, and God's Creation isn't limited to physical objects. The laws of science we've learned were created by God, as well as the forces of electricity, magnetism, and gravity. The sheer scope of what Creation truly encompasses can be dizzying to think about. One description is found in John 1:3, "All things came into being through God, and without God not one thing came into being."

Not only physical objects and the forces of the universe, but also everyone who exists, or has or will exist, comes from God. From the most famous of saints to the most quickly forgotten kindly neighbor; from the kid who shoplifts gum in a gas station to the serial killer. This can be difficult for us to imagine in another way. When a natural disaster strikes, we can often realize that the laws of science which govern nature, while created by God, were not created specifically to destroy that one area at that specific time. When one person hurts another, we feel it far more personally. "Did God want this to happen?" is a common question in the face of human-caused tragedy. We might ask, did we earn this?

Of course, humanity is one of the most recent aspects of God's Creation. The whole of human history is just an eyeblink long, compared to the length of time the rest of Creation existed before us. So, as illustrated in the Creation stories of Genesis, we've been given the stewardship of Creation without having earned it; a gift freely given. When asked if a blind man or his parents had sinned and somehow caused him to be born blind, Jesus responded in John 9, "Neither this man nor his parents sinned; he was born blind so that God's works might be revealed in him." God is at work all through Creation, and while God does not cause tragedies intentionally, still God can bring about hope and grace in tragic situations.

1. What object in your life has most irritated you in the last week? What materials that God created is it made of? How many years of studying Creation did it take for us to learn to make it?

This week I will pray for:

Jesus Christ

Reading: Philippians 2:5-11

Hymn: O Sacred Head Now Wounded ELW 351

Jesus' Life

We have four Gospels that tell us the story of Jesus' life and ministry on earth. Each Gospel has a different emphasis. Mark was the first written, and tells the story in a rushed, hurried way. One imagines the author was eager to get the story written down. Matthew and Luke were written later, around the same time. Matthew was written specifically to the new Christians of the time who had come from the Jewish faith and references the Hebrew Scriptures often. Luke was written to the *Gentiles* (non-Jews) and focuses on the less powerful people who are present in Jesus' life: Gentiles, women, and outcasts. John was written last and focuses on explaining doctrine. Each Gospel is a little different, but as they were all written many years after the Resurrection, that's not surprising.

Coming to us as one of us was not the backup plan, and Jesus' time with us was foretold long before the first Christmas. The Gospel of Matthew points out many of the prophecies that Jesus' time on earth fulfilled. Also, that first Christmas was when Jesus was born as a human, but that was not the beginning of his existence. The Athanasian Creed explains that Jesus, fully equal with

God the Creator and the Holy Spirit, was co-eternal with them and has always existed. The Messiah is mentioned many times in the Hebrew Scriptures as existing but not yet arrived.

The "Christ Hymn" in Philippians speaks of Christ emptying himself for us by coming to us as a human being. While Jesus was clearly divine during his time on earth, he was still subject to the normal parts of a human life. He ate, slept, went through puberty, and probably got the occasional cold, or stepped on a nail in the workshop. He was fully both human and divine - 100% and 100%, not 50/50.

1. Often those who are just starting to learn about the Christian faith ask where in the Bible they should start reading, and the Gospels are a common suggestion. Given their differences, which of the four would you suggest a new Christian start with?

Jesus' Death & Resurrection

Why did Jesus have to die? Why was he crucified? These are normal questions to ask when hearing the stories of Holy Week. Since Jesus was fully human, he would have died of old age, if nothing else. But instead he was crucified by the Romans, occupying Israel, who saw him as a political threat to their power. Once he claimed the title of Messiah of Israel, that was a direct challenge to the legitimacy of their rule, and he was executed for treason the traditional way - crucifixion. As Christians, we also claim in faith that something else was going on. That Jesus Christ was the Lamb of God who died for our sins, whose body and blood were shed for us. When we receive communion, we confess that God's love for us has no limits, even to death itself, because that is how far God went to prove God's love for us.

Crucifixion was such a painful and insulting death, that Roman citizens could not be executed that way as a privilege of their citizenship. Once they arrived at the place of crucifixion, the cross would have been laid down on the ground, and Jesus would have been laid down on top of it. Each arm would have first been tied tightly to the arms of the cross, and his lower legs would have been tied to the central post, so once the cross was upright, the rope would take some of his weight. The nails used would have been large, and driven separately through each wrist and ankle, as the hands and feet aren't strong enough to take that much weight for that long. Then the cross would be pulled upright and the bottom of the post would be a few feet deep in the ground. Death was not usually caused by blood loss, but by suffocation. After several hours on a cross, the body simply cannot hold itself upright anymore and will droop forward, and that combined with increasing exhaustion makes it very difficult to breathe. If a criminal had not died after a certain amount of time, their legs would be broken to hasten their death. Artwork of the crucifixion will often take some artistic license with how the scene is portrayed.

Jesus did both fully die and was completely resurrected back to life afterwards. While some have suggested that maybe the Resurrection wasn't "real" and perhaps Jesus was in a coma, or simply very near death when laid in the tomb and recovered naturally, this is so unlikely as to be impossible. The Roman soldiers crucifying Jesus would have known how to check if a person was truly dead and lying in a sealed tomb for three days would not make a person who was near death any healthier. In the same way, Jesus was also fully brought back to life, and was not undead, or a zombie. There are descriptions of his body in the Bible after the resurrection that show this - he was healthy and ate like anyone else.

1. What did Jesus do when he saw his friends the disciples again, after he was resurrected, in Luke 24? Would that have been your first choice too?

Jesus Today

What does Jesus mean for us today? First, that sin has no power over us. Jesus' life, death, and resurrection redeemed us from the consequences of our sin. Do we still sin? Yes, we are not perfect, and we do break our relationship with God and others (that is, sin). That may have consequences for us in our daily lives. But God's love for us is more powerful than our sin, and God's grace washes us clean of our sin in our baptism, when we receive communion, and when we confess and ask forgiveness.

Second, Jesus' life, death, and resurrection, means death has no power over us. Our bodies will die, but we are then commended to God's care, and at the end of time, as proclaimed in the Apostles' Creed, there will be a bodily resurrection of all the saints, as described in Revelation. Jesus has overcome the power of death and therefore we have no need to fear death. Indeed, we have no reason to doubt God's love for us, because God has been one of us. God has gone through the same troubles we have and understands humanity as only another human could. And yet God loves us still.

The cross is often central to Christian worship and is displayed in many shapes. For example:

- **The Empty Cross**: Jesus has risen!
- **The Crucifix**: Jesus on the cross, for us.
- **The Celtic Cross**: The cross stretches over the world (the circle).
- **The Jerusalem Cross**: Symbol of the Christian journey (cross among crossroads).

1. Do you have different crosses in your life? What do they mean for you?

This week I will pray for:

Holy Spirit

Reading: Matthew 3:11-17

Hymn: Spirit of Gentleness ELW 396

Bible & Holy Spirit

We've discussed God the Creator, and Jesus Christ the Redeemer. Now we arrive at the Holy Spirit, the Sanctifier (*sank-tih-fire*). To *sanctify* means to make holy, and that's what the Holy Spirit does. God surrounds us in Creation, and Jesus is with us in the sacraments and in our hearts, but it's the Holy Spirit that is constantly at work around us in the world, showering God's gifts on us and making us holy. The Spirit inspires us to do God's work in the world and share God's love with others.

The Holy Spirit appears throughout the Bible. Genesis 1:2 is often translated as the Spirit of God moving over the waters. Several of the prophets speak of the Spirit, including Joel and Isaiah. But the Holy Spirit is more clearly discussed in the New Testament. While the Spirit appears in the Gospels several times, it seems especially active in the book of Acts, and Paul speaks about it extensively in his letters. Some gifts of the Spirit are listed more specifically in Galatians 5:22-23, "...the fruit of the Spirit is love, joy, peace, patience, kindness, generosity, faithfulness, gentleness, and self-control." During difficult times in our lives, we may reach out to God

49

for one of these gifts. Prayer helps us better recognize the Holy Spirit in our lives and encourages these gifts.

Some people choose to refer to the Holy Spirit with feminine pronouns - "she" and "her." This is because in Hebrew, which most of the Hebrew Scriptures are written in, and in Aramaic, the language Jesus spoke which also appears extensively in the Hebrew Scriptures, nouns are given a gender. (Many other languages do this today, such as Spanish.) Both the Hebrew and Aramaic words for "Spirit" are feminine nouns. Greek, the language of the New Testament, also gives genders to nouns: masculine, feminine, and neuter. The word for "Spirit" in Greek is neuter. Since English does not give gender to nouns, the first translators used masculine pronouns to refer to the Spirit because they assumed anything that powerful must be male in nature. But for us today, as the Holy Spirit does not have a gender, which pronouns to use is a matter of personal choice.

1. Which of the gifts or fruits of the Spirit do you most appreciate in others, and why? Which one do you wish you had more of? What would your life be like if you did?

Church & Holy Spirit

As discussed in "Season of Pentecost Holidays," the Holy Spirit played an active role in the beginning of the church. When the Spirit descended on the disciples at Pentecost, giving them the ability to speak in different languages, this led to the baptism of over 3,000 people who heard the disciples preach the Gospel. As a result, Pentecost is often called the "Birthday of the Church." The Holy Spirit still has an active role in the workings of the church, which can be seen in many ways. Church meetings will ask for the guidance of the Spirit in prayer, as will many small group Bible studies.

The Spirit continues to work in us through worship, prayer, and the preaching of the Gospel, today.

The Holy Spirit is also at work in the sacraments of baptism and communion. When the water for baptism is blessed, it is the Holy Spirit who sanctifies it. As in the story of Jesus' baptism in the Gospels, it is the Spirit who descends upon the baptized, and marks them with the cross of Christ forever. When the wine and bread are blessed for communion, that is again the Holy Spirit. The Spirit makes us holy through the sacraments and plays a constant, active role in our lives through them. Through our baptism, the Spirit encourages our faith daily and nurtures our relationship with God and the church. Through communion, the Spirit shares God's grace and love with us, and reminds us that we are connected to all Christians and equal with them in the eyes of God.

Just as the Holy Spirit gathers and keeps the church now, this will always be the Spirit's role, even through and after the end of time. As discussed more thoroughly in "The End of All Things," after Jesus returns in the Second Coming, there will be a bodily (not as ghosts but in physical bodies) resurrection, and the last judgment, which involves purifying us and removing our brokenness, and reconciling our relationship with God. That resurrection and final gathering of the church will be the work of the Holy Spirit, who will then gather us for the final, eternal worship service when we will sing praises to God in heaven, as described in Revelation.

1. Prayer is one of the many ways the Spirit works in our lives, including prayers we might dismiss as "routine" - table prayers, for example. Have you ever silently added to a table prayer, perhaps asking for peaceful conversation during a meal or reconciliation?

You & Holy Spirit

Sometimes when we talk about faith, we make it sound like one of the muscles in our bodies. We "exercise" our faith by being a part of a community of believers, and how we choose to act. We have "strong" or "weak" faith at different points in our lives. We "nurture" our faith by attending church and reading the Bible and praying. When we talk in this way, it might sound like our faith is something we have total control over, which can lead to thinking that any weakness or difficulty in our faith is a personal failing, even a moral failing, making us a bad person.

But this is not true: just as our muscles and body are a gift from God, our faith is also a gift, given through the Holy Spirit (see 1st Corinthians 12:3). These gifts from God don't always work as we expect or even want them to, as those with physical disabilities or chronic illnesses can tell us. But problems with them are not moral failings or even something we have perfect control over. We can take care of our bodies as best we can through diet and exercise, and in the same way we can take care of our faith through worship, prayer, and Bible study.

Just as our body might not always be as we'd prefer - we may be lactose intolerant, or diabetic, or have fibromyalgia, or muscular dystrophy - our faith might feel tired, or hurt, or somehow incomplete at times. This is where the church comes in. Just as medical science can help us with our bodies through medication or tools, from antidepressants to wheelchairs, the Holy Spirit works through our fellow Christians to support us in our faith. When our faith needs encouragement, solitary prayer and Bible study are not our only options. We can seek encouragement through worship, or in church groups. We can turn to a pastor or trusted Christian friend. A day serving at a soup kitchen with the youth group, or a trip to church camp or a National Youth Gathering, can be places to encounter the Holy Spirit in a powerful way.

1. Can you name one person you're not related to, other than your pastor, who you could turn to if you needed encouragement in your faith? Would you welcome that person if they came to you?

This week I will pray for:

Small Catechism: Lord's Prayer

Teach Us to Pray

Reading: Matthew 6:1-8

Hymn: Lord's Prayer ELW s163

Why We Pray

Could you be friends with someone and never talk to them? You could like them all right, and not do anything to hurt them, and maybe even smile at them once in a while. Imagine trying to be friends with someone and never talking, emailing, texting, or otherwise communicating with them. How long do you think that friendship would last? How deep do you think it would be? In the same way, while it might be possible to be Christian and never pray, that's not ideal. Prayer helps us in so many ways - it strengthens our relationship with God, it helps us to realize what's truly important, and it gives God yet another way to offer us wisdom and comfort. Besides, we have an always-open, direct line to the God who created everything from atoms to galaxies; why wouldn't we use it?

We pray in many ways and for different purposes. Sometimes, especially during worship, we pray together. Sometimes just one person will be speaking, sometimes the whole group will speak aloud together. This is called *corporate* prayer, because the group is praying together even if only one is speaking aloud. We also pray on our own, as individuals, either spoken or silently. Sometimes our prayer is formal and planned, sometimes it's informal and off-the-cuff. Our prayers will have different purposes: maybe we're looking for guidance, or we're giving thanks, or we're confessing to something.

One of the most familiar types of corporate prayer to many Lutherans, other than the Lord's Prayer, is the Confession & Forgiveness that begins most worship services. We begin by *invoking* God, or calling on God. Then there's a short prayer acknowledging God's grace and power in our lives. The confession itself is usually pre-written so that all those worshiping can recite it together (including those leading the service!), and because of that it's often in general terms, rather than specific. At the end of this we directly ask God for forgiveness. Finally, the worship leader declares God's forgiveness of our sins.

If a person is struggling with a sin, and corporate confession or individual prayer isn't helping them in that struggle, private confession between the person and a pastor is an option. It's not that common in some Lutheran congregations but it is always available. The pastor is bound by strict laws of confidentiality to not share anything discussed during the confession unless there is a legal issue of *mandated reporting*, which is usually the case if someone is in immediate danger. (Mandated reporting laws vary from state to state and can be researched on the internet.)

1. What do you talk about with your family? With your friends? With your youth group? With God?

How We Pray

We don't always pray using a pre-written prayer, so it can be helpful to have a guide to follow when we're praying in our own words. An easy-to-remember acronym can be a useful guide. ACTS stands for **A**doration (praising God) **C**onfession (of sin) **T**hanksgiving (for blessings) **S**upplication (asking for help). PRAY stands for **P**raise (God) **R**epent (from sin) **A**sk (for help) **Y**ield (to God's answer). Or your prayer can be guided by your hand with the Five Finger prayer: touch the Thumb as you pray for those *closest* to you, the Pointer finger for those who *point* you in the right direction, the Tallest finger for those in *authority*, the Ring finger for those who are *sick or in need*, and the Pinkie finger for *your own* needs and concerns.

What do we do with our body while we pray? There are lots of poses people take while praying, and most of them are meant to help us focus on our prayer and shut off from other concerns. Many people close their eyes while they pray to do just that. In medieval times, it was common to lie face down on the floor with your arms spread out like Jesus on the cross, if you were asking God for something important. These days we might kneel, to show our humility to God, or stand at attention to show respect (like we do with the flag). We can fold our hands to keep ourselves from fidgeting so we can focus better, or we can open our arms & hands up to heaven to show we welcome God's love and wisdom. There's really only one absolute rule of what to do with your body when you pray: if you're doing anything dangerous while praying, such as driving or chopping vegetables or supervising small children, your eyes must stay open!

Sometimes, the question of "when do we pray" has an obvious answer: during worship, before meals, before bed. But there are many other options. Sometimes we pray because of what is happening at the moment - if you see an ambulance pass you can pray for those in it, or if you see an accident happen. Sometimes we pray because we're asked to - if someone asks you to pray for them, a good way to make sure you won't forget is to do it right away! Sometimes we don't realize we're praying until we're halfway through - maybe you were just thinking to yourself and suddenly you realize you were really talking to God the whole time. We can pray no matter what kind of mood we're in - when we're happy, or sad, or angry at God or at another person, or confused. Prayer is something we can do pretty much anywhere, and at any time.

1. What were you up to the last time you prayed informally? Was something happening?

Prayer in the Bible

The Psalms are often called the prayer book of the Bible. Have you ever wanted to pray but didn't feel like you could find the words you wanted to say? At times like that it can be helpful to page through the Psalms, where you will find many heartfelt and vivid prayers written. Even though they were written a long time ago, and some of the imagery might surprise us, they still seem very appropriate and familiar in some ways, don't they? Perhaps what people are praying for now hasn't changed that much from what they prayed for thousands of years ago. The Psalms are often also called the hymnbook of the Bible, because they can be sung, too. Many Christians especially enjoy praying through music, whether that's through the Psalms or hymns or praise songs.

There are many times that Jesus prays throughout the Gospels. He prays at various times for healing for the sick, for his disciples and followers, and sometimes we read that he prays but we don't know what he was praying about. This can be a good reminder for us that, just as we don't always know what Jesus was praying for, we also don't always know what our friends and family are praying for. When we pray for the people we care about, we can also ask God to answer their prayers that we don't know about- just because we don't know all their troubles doesn't mean we can't ask for God's help with them.

Lectio Divina is an ancient practice of "praying through the Bible." Let's try it in class!

1. One of Jesus' most memorable prayers is when he prayed in the Garden of Gethsemane, for "this cup to be taken." (Matthew 26:36-39) Does this prayer change how you think about Jesus?

This week I will pray for:

Addressing God

Reading: Deuteronomy 6:4-9

Hymn: Mothering God ELW 735

Our Father, Hallowed Be

Why does the Lord's Prayer start with "*Our* Father"? Sometimes we say it alone, when that happens shouldn't we say "*My* Father?" But by saying *our*, we are always reminded that we are not alone in our faith, and we are surrounded by children of God around the world. In the same way, starting the prayer by calling God "Father" instead of "Almighty" or "Everlasting" reminds us that our relationship with God is a family relationship. The love and trust and communication we have with God, is an illustration of the best that a family can be. God wants us to say Father in confidence and trust and speak with the same honesty and love that a nurturing, healthy family offers. This can especially comfort those whose family is troubled - no matter what, we all have a Father who always cares and pays attention.

What does "Hallowed be thy name" mean, anyway? If something is *hallowed*, that's another way of saying it's treated as holy or sacred. *Hallowing* people and things - making them holy - is the Holy Spirit's job. Another way to say, "Hallowed be thy name" is "May your name be treated in a holy way," - by us, humanity. God's name is holy in itself; that's why we have the 2nd Commandment. When we treat God's name as a holy word, it reminds us of God's role in our lives, and our own holiness in God's eyes.

How does God's name become hallowed among us? The sharing of the Gospel and the teaching of the word of God, leads us to live holy lives and to share God's love with others. This is how God's name becomes truly holy among us. This isn't about just *not* using God's name as a curse word. If God's name is truly treated as holy, in the church, then everything we do will be shaped by that. We will be inspired to act with kindness and generosity, with compassion and mercy, to everyone we meet, and to truly see each of our neighbors as beloved children of God, and our equals.

1. Think back over the last week, of when God's name (God, Jesus, etc.) was spoken around you, whether in person or on TV, etc. What emotions were being shared when God's name was used? If your name was constantly used that way, how would it inspire other people to treat you?

Kingdom Come

When the Bible talks about "the kingdom of God," what do you think of? Heaven? Life after death? Some kind of reference to after the end of the world when God will have even more obvious control over things than right now? Often when we use the phrase, it does sound like it's interchangeable with any or all of these - but really it refers to something completely different. Something that's going on right now, that we are surrounded by, and adding to ourselves, all the time.

The kingdom of God is right here with us, right now, and it's something we are building ourselves, with God's help! Remember how if we treat God's name as holy, then everything we do will be shaped by that? This is the kingdom of God - it's the church doing God's work in the world, sharing God with others, encouraging God's influence on our society. When we pray, "Your kingdom come," we're asking, "Help us to be more like you, God, more forgiving, loving, and compassionate, so we can inspire others to be like that too, and change the world." As the kingdom of God becomes stronger in the world, the more holy we become, and the more God's influence is felt by those who need it most.

If we stopped praying the Lord's Prayer tomorrow, and stopped praying for God's kingdom to come entirely - would it stop? No, of course not! God is working on this through us whether or not we pray for it. Our prayers for this aren't about reminding God of an item on the Divine To-Do List, or bullying God into doing what we want. (We might try, but it doesn't work.) Instead our prayers do two things: they encourage our relationship with God, as discussed above, and they help us to prioritize our own kingdom-building work.

Think about it - have you ever gone to pray for something, and realized that really, you weren't comfortable talking to God about it, the way you talked to your friends or family about it? Have you ever gone to God with something you wanted, and suddenly when you say it in prayer it sounds selfish or unimportant? Have you ever prayed about someone and realized, as you said the prayer, that the way you were talking about them wasn't really as forgiving or compassionate as you could be? This is the Holy Spirit, building God's kingdom in our hearts. When we pray about something or someone, often it helps us to see what's truly important. And that helps us make decisions in our everyday lives.

1. Is it easier to be generous and forgiving to others when you're having a good day, than a bad day? Have you ever tried to make someone's day better in the hopes they'll be nicer to you? What does this tell us about how to go about building the kingdom of God?

Will Be Done

In the Small Catechism the Lord's Prayer is broken up into *petitions*, which are separate statements and requests to God. The Third Petition is "Your will be done, on earth as it is in heaven." When we say the Lord's Prayer out loud, we sometimes break it up differently, as though "Your kingdom come" and "Your will be done" go together as one thought. But really "Your kingdom come" is one thought - a hope, a prayer - and "Your will be done on earth as it is in heaven" works more as a reminder for us. After all, God's will is easily done in heaven - no one's objecting there. It's harder for God's will to get done on Earth, where sin and suffering and conflicting interests get in the way. Again, just like with God's kingdom being built, this wouldn't stop if we suddenly stopped praying it, but we do want this reminder, so we continue to pray it.

This is a reminder we need, too! So often we get caught up in what we want, what our family wants, and what our friends (and the people we wish were our friends) want. We can forget to ask, is this the right thing to do? Is this the generous and compassionate and loving thing to do? Is this what God would want me to do? So, when we pray the Lord's Prayer, we remind ourselves to ask those questions. The more we ask these questions, the easier it is for us to continue to build God's kingdom in the world.

It also reminds us that the world isn't supposed to work the way we want it to, it's supposed to work the way God wants it to - as God's kingdom. God's kingdom isn't perfect yet, we're still building it. God is always working against evil and suffering in the world, but evil and suffering still exist. When we talk about God's will, it's important to remember that God does not set out to punish us, through illness, disaster, or other kinds of suffering. Check out John 9:1-3, when Jesus says so, and then declares God's work is shown through a blind man - before he's healed! God's will comes about in unexpected ways.

1. What do you think a "perfect world" according to what you want, would look like? What do you think a "perfect world" according to what God wants, would look like? What are some differences?

This week I will pray for:

Our Needs

Reading: Psalm 23

Hymn: Joyful, Joyful We Adore Thee ELW 836

Daily Bread

What do we need? In 1943, a psychologist named Abraham Maslow developed a pyramid of human needs. The needs towards the bottom are fundamental for survival, and the needs at the top are necessary for a full and happy life. We start with physical needs such as food, water, and shelter, and basic safety from danger. Then a sense of belonging, whether through friends, family, or larger community. Next respect, which can also be called esteem, from others in our community and for ourselves. And finally having joy and being fulfilled by having a sense of purpose in what we do.

All of these things are needs for the kind of life God hopes we will live. And God has put all of these things within our reach. The world has plenty of resources and farmland to feed the entire population of the world. At this point, what is stopping us from no one going hungry ever again? Distribution of those resources - or put more plainly, greed. When some people take far more than they will ever need, then others who are more vulnerable suffer. This goes for food, water, or any other kind of resource. The Earth can meet everyone's physical needs. The only thing stopping us is human greed.

The other needs are also based on how we treat one another. Safety comes from a trusted community and looking out for each other. Belonging comes from welcoming one another and being in fellowship. Esteem and respect are the way that God calls us to treat one another. Fulfillment comes to us through our vocation, or what God calls us to do with our lives, whether that is a paid career or not.

When we pray, "Give us this day our daily bread," we remind ourselves that God has provided us with the ability for everyone to have what they need, and we ask God to show us the differences between what we truly need, and what we want. Knowing this helps us to make decisions in our lives. Especially, it reminds us to make sure that others have their daily needs, whether they are our close neighbors or live further away.

1. When we look at the world, we see that daily needs are not provided for by God on a merit basis. We see people who do good things in trouble, and people who do bad things doing well. Do you think God should provide for only "good" people? What makes a person good?

Forgiving Trespasses

There are at least three English versions of the Lord's Prayer, and the line about forgiveness might refer to either "debts," "trespasses," or "sins." A debt is when you owe something to someone. It's not always money; it could be a favor, or it might be that you hurt someone and want to make it up to them. A trespass doesn't always involve trespassing on property; it might involve intruding, overstepping, or meddling in some way. A debt or trespass could be emotional, spiritual, or boundaries related.

Sometimes we talk about sin, as a general concept, and sometimes we talk about specific sins. Sin is the state of our relationship with God; the relationship is broken, and the chasm between us and God is sin. If there was no sin in the world, we'd all be in perfect relationship with God all the time. Individual sins, whether they are specific acts or general tendencies we have (lying, or a tendency to lie) show us the impact that sin has on the world, and on us.

As Christians we don't believe we can earn God's forgiveness. There's no one formula or action we can do that will automatically mean we "deserve" to be forgiven by God. Any debts or trespasses or sins we've done, we might be able to fix some of the consequences for, but they still happened and can't be completely erased. So instead we rely on God's grace, which is forgiveness given freely.

But we also know that our forgiveness by God, is connected to our ability to forgive others who have a debt to us or have trespassed or sinned against us. If we believe we are forgiven, we will find it's easier to forgive others. If we understand what forgiveness means and looks like from God, it's easier to see and encourage it in others around us. But it also goes the other way - a person who hasn't experienced being forgiven, will probably find it harder to forgive others. So, God tells us to forgive one another as God has forgiven us. (See Luke 6:37 and Matthew 6:14.)

1. We can't earn or deserve God's forgiveness. Can we earn or deserve a person's forgiveness?

Temptation & Evil

We're constantly surrounded by temptations - like greed, hatred, or contempt- and each of us has some temptations that are stronger for us than others. Being tempted happens to everyone, and the experience of being tempted itself, isn't a sin. Luther called this being "attacked" by temptation, and you don't consent to being attacked. The question is whether we will give in to the temptation to be selfish, or bigoted, or conceited, or the other various temptations that surround us. God doesn't lead us to these temptations, which come from sin, but God can help lead us away from them. This is what we ask when we pray the Lord's Prayer. Of course, it's easier to avoid temptation when we can recognize it for what it is. We can also ask God's help in that when we pray, but a strong, encouraging Christian community can help us recognize and avoid many temptations.

When we ask God to deliver us from evil, we're summing up the whole Lord's Prayer. We've asked God already to help us treat God's name as holy, to bring about God's kingdom, to provide for our daily needs, to help us to forgive, and to keep us from temptation. All of these are ways of delivering us from different kinds of evil. Treating God's name as holy keeps us from idolatry and irreverence; kingdom building keeps us from selfishness; having our daily needs met keeps us from poverty and fear; forgiveness keeps us from hatred; and avoiding temptation keeps us from many kinds of sin. But when we ask God to deliver us from evil, we mean all kinds of evil - suffering, violence, and death, among others.

If you've ever prayed the Lord's Prayer with Catholics, you've noticed Lutherans pray an additional line at the end of the Lord's Prayer. This is because of a disagreement about exactly what the original version of Matthew 6:13 said. When we pray that kingdom, power, and glory are God's forever, we're reminding ourselves that God does hear our prayers and will answer them. (Whether or not we will like the answer is another question entirely.) We don't pray because other people tell us to, or because we think we're supposed to, but because we believe that our prayers matter to God, and that God pays attention to them and to us. We double down on this again when we say "Amen" at the end of our prayers. The word "Amen" means "yes, I believe this is absolutely true."

1. Think about a few times you've been tempted in the last couple of months. You don't need to get specific, but what types of temptation have you faced? Greed, violence, contempt, lying, pride?

This week I will pray for:

Small Catechism: Sacraments

Communion: What God Does

Reading: Luke 22:14-27

Hymn: You Satisfy the Hungry Heart ELW 484

Elements, Commands & Grace

The Lutheran church celebrates two *sacraments*, or visible signs of God's grace: baptism and communion. According to Martin Luther, there are three necessary criteria for a sacrament: there must be physical elements involved, we must be commanded to do so by Jesus in the Bible, and it must convey God's grace. In communion, the physical elements are the bread and wine. The Christian church has had many traditions surrounding the bread and wine, which will be discussed in *Communion: What We Do.*

Jesus' command to the disciples to take communion occurs in the Last Supper story as told in the Gospels of Matthew, Mark, and Luke. (John does not contain the Words of Institution, but Jesus' "I am the bread of life" speech in chapter 6 has this command as well.) We can see in 1 Corinthians that this instruction was understood to not just be for the 12 disciples but for all Christians. When Paul, the author of the letter, quotes the Words of Institution from the Gospels, the following verse is addressed to all his readers: "For as often as you eat this bread and drink the cup, you proclaim the Lord's death until he comes." (1 Corinthians 11:26) That proclamation is one of the main missions of the church.

The grace given through communion is mentioned in each of the three stories of the first communion at the Last Supper, for example in Matthew 26:27-28, "Drink from it, all of you; for this is my blood of the covenant, which is poured out for many for the forgiveness of sins." Jesus does not put any qualifications on that grace: it's not necessary to specifically confess to each individual sin you've committed in order to obtain this grace (Luther tried that, it takes quite a while); this is a gift to all Christians. The church has also had many practices for when and how often to take communion, which will also be discussed in *Communion: What We Do.*

1. Jesus gives several instructions to his disciples which we understand to apply to us as well. Think about the Bible stories you know of Jesus teaching the disciples: what might some examples be?

In, With & Under

We use many names for communion: Holy Communion, the Lord's Supper, the Eucharist, or the Mass. When we call this sacrament Holy Communion, we emphasize that this is not just a way that we *commune* with (have close relationship with) God, but also that we do so in community. Communion, commune, and community are all related words. When we call this sacrament the Lord's Supper, we remind ourselves of the Last Supper on Maundy Thursday. The word "Eucharist" comes from a Greek word that means thanksgiving, and it reminds us that this is a way to give thanks for Jesus' sacrifice and also for the gifts of creation represented in the bread and wine. The word "Mass," often used for a service of word and sacrament by the Roman Catholic Church, comes from a Latin word for dismissal. It refers to when the congregation is sent out, having been fed by worship, to share the love of God with the world.

As Lutherans, we believe that Jesus Christ himself is truly present in the bread and wine at communion, as he said, "this is my body," and "this is my blood." We aren't just remembering Jesus' sacrifice for us, he is truly right there with us, in the elements. Luther phrased it that Jesus is "in, with, and under" the elements. There is a story of Luther discussing Christ's real presence in the elements at communion with another theologian, Zwingli, who disagreed with him. They had this conversation over several days, going through Bible verses and books written about communion as they argued. Finally, one day Zwingli asked Luther what he meant, when he said that Jesus *is* in the bread and wine. Luther had prepared for this and pulled the tablecloth off the table they were using (scattering books and papers everywhere!) and showed Zwingli the word "IS" that he had carved into the wooden table.

This puts Lutherans in something of a middle ground when it comes to how we understand communion, compared to Catholics and Baptists, for example. Catholics believe that the bread and wine are miraculously changed into Christ's whole presence (common phrase: 'body, blood, soul, and divinity') while the appearances of bread and wine remain. So, the bread and wine are no longer present - only Jesus veiled under the appearances of bread and wine. (The official term for this is *transubstantiation*, as opposed to Luther's *consubstantiation*, but you aren't expected to remember either of those.) Baptists, on the other hand, understand communion to be a reenactment of the Last Supper and a memorial to Jesus' sacrifice, but do not believe that Jesus is any more or less present in communion than anywhere else.

1. Given what you've learned, what do you think the word "Christmas" (Christ-Mass) really means?

Body of Christ

Sometimes, when speaking about communion, we say that "we receive what we are." We receive the body of Christ in communion in the bread and wine, and we also understand that we, Christ's church, are also the body of Christ in the world. It is our hands and feet that do the work of God, our voices that encourage others to respond to the Holy Spirit, our actions that show the love of God to all people. This is how we acknowledge that what we do in this life matters, because we are a vital and necessary part of God's work. We also speak of being the body of Christ as a way of speaking about the unity of the Christian church. We all have different gifts, each denomination emphasizes different characteristics of God, but just as a body has many different parts, but is still one, so we are one while still individuals.

As a way of showing this unity to others, the ELCA practices what we call eucharistic hospitality, or open table communion. All baptized Christians are welcome to receive communion at any ELCA congregation, because the communion table belongs to Jesus Christ, not to us, and Jesus extended his invitation to all Christians. However we do also understand that not everyone may feel comfortable receiving communion at an ELCA congregation because of their own religious convictions, as some Christians do not practice open table communion, and others wait longer than we do to allow children their first communion. As a way of extending hospitality without asking them to deny their convictions, a blessing is extended. (Or for a person of another religion who was willing to accept a blessing.)

The Christian church has not been entirely unified for a thousand years, and we long for the day when it will be again. In an effort to bring that about, the ELCA engages in dialogues with other denominations, attempting to bring about full communion agreements where possible. However, we do still honor the convictions of those who we are not in full communion with; and when visiting a congregation in a denomination that we do not have such an agreement with, we respect their traditions by asking permission to take communion. We are in full communion agreements with the Presbyterian Church USA, Reformed Church in America, United Church of Christ, Episcopal Church, Moravian Church, and the United Methodist Church, as well as all members of the Lutheran World Federation.

1. What do you have in common with all of the body of Christ? What makes you unique?

This week I will pray for:

Communion: What We Do

Reading: Luke 8:42b-48

Hymn: Soul Adorn Yourself With Gladness ELW 488

Preparation for the Table

Perhaps you've attended a worship service that ran a little longer than usual, and wondered why all those pieces of the service were included? The Lutheran worship service is designed to prepare the congregation to receive communion! Two parts of the service are particularly geared towards getting us ready for the sacrament: the order of confession, and the sharing of the peace. As you've read, one of the things that communion does is convey God's grace. The order of confession and forgiveness at the start of the service reminds us not only that we are in need of that grace, but also that God's forgiveness is truly offered to us. We share the peace before receiving communion because of Jesus' instructions to us in Matthew 5:23, where he says that any person who arrives at a service to worship God, who has an argument going with someone, needs to go make peace with that person. The sharing of the peace isn't just a time to greet one another, it's a chance for those with disagreements to approach one another in Christian love and heal their relationship.

But what if you arrive at a service late (it does happen) and you miss those parts of the service? Can you still take communion? The answer is yes! The preparation we go through early in the service is good and helpful for us, but any baptized and believing Christian is always welcome at the table.

Another part of our preparation is that we always keep proclamation of the word and celebration of the sacrament together, they go hand in hand. We read from the scriptures and we pray for those in need as a part of the communion service, because receiving God's grace is always accompanied by hearing God's word, and showing care for creation and our fellow children of God through prayer. If we just had communion, we might miss an opportunity to gain further understanding through God's word, or to be spurred to action to help others through prayer. All of these pieces are an important part of worship. It's also natural that the entire congregation participates in the service, as far as they are able. Having members of the congregation read the scripture, share music, pass the offering plates, greet the worshipers, serve as acolyte, or assist in serving communion, is one of the ways we make visible that all Christians have important roles to play in the ministry of the church.

1. Have you ever shared the peace with someone you didn't like? (No names!) What was it like?

Bread & Wine (or Grape Juice?)

We speak about the bread and wine of communion, but it turns out there are a lot of types of bread and wine, so that covers a lot of ground! There are many traditions of exactly which types to use. Some congregations prefer to use the "common loaf" and each person receives a pinch of baked bread from the same loaf. Some prefer to use wafers, which don't get stale as quickly as regular bread does. As there are people with allergies or dietary restrictions (such as celiac disease) which require them to avoid certain ingredients, some congregation choose the wafers (which include only flour and water as ingredients), or provide a gluten-free option. There are also Christians who live in parts of the world where wheat is not commonly available, and so they might use bread made of a different grain, perhaps rice or barley. Congregations may include recovering alcoholics or those with medical conditions that do not allow them to have any alcohol, and therefore offer grape juice as an alternative. In fact some Christian denominations offer only grape juice as a matter of course, as they hold that drinking alcohol is not a Christian act. The wine or juice may be served through a common cup, through intinction, or through small personal cups, depending on local tradition. If a person can't receive one of the elements offered, for whatever reason, receiving one element is just as effective as both.

Whatever types of bread or wine (or grape juice) that are offered, they are treated with care & reverence once they have been blessed. Leftover bread and wine may be disposed of in a few ways. If the congregation uses wafers, the leftovers are stored and used for visitation to those who could not attend the service, or perhaps kept until the next time communion is offered. Leftover bread may be eaten by the assembly or scattered outside to feed the local wildlife and be returned to God's creation that way. Leftover wine may be drunk by the assembly; poured into the ground (dirt if at all possible) to be returned to the lifecycle of creation; or if hygienic facilities exist, stored until able to be used.

The whole process of communion is completed with unity & dignity. Distribution is offered to the entire assembly and the words used during distribution reflect the equality of all present. All worshipers receive communion during the same period of the service, and those who cannot physically reach the area where distribution is taking place, have communion brought to them. Those who are waiting to receive or who have received already show their devotion through either participating in a shared hymn or silent prayer.

1. Why does it matter that the whole worshiping assembly is offered communion at the same time?

Communion & Community

How often communion is received varies by congregation. The tradition of receiving communion weekly was established by the Roman Catholic Church before the Reformation. It is normal in European countries to receive communion weekly in many denominations. In some areas of the world where pastors cover larger geographic areas compared to Europe, which is densely populated, congregations receive communion less often. During the 1800's in the western United States, isolated congregations would receive communion when a circuit rider pastor, traveling between several congregations, came to town, a few times a year. Congregations are encouraged to celebrate communion weekly and on festivals in order to reinforce the gifts which communion brings - God's grace and as a reminder of our life in community.

Congregations also vary on how old children need to be to receive their First Communion. Some do communion education first and may wait until confirmation, others give communion to any baptized child physically able to receive it and education is continuous. These policies are often informed by the treatment of other groups. For example, a person with Alzheimer's is often able to receive communion through several stages of the disease. An adult being baptized is welcome to receive communion at their baptism, with the understanding their education will continue. Common choices for First Communion ages are 7 and 10, with some congregations inviting parents to decide when their child is ready.

Communion is not a secret ceremony or a private ritual. The congregation receives communion at services which are open to all the baptized, and private groups are discouraged from having communion when it wouldn't be possible for any Christian passing by to join them. Communion is taken to those in hospitals, nursing homes, or prisons, but any Christian present is always invited to take part.

1. Have you ever received communion more than once in a week? More than once in a day?

This week I will pray for:

Baptism: What God Does

Reading: Romans 6:1-11

Hymn: Awake O Sleeper Rise from Death ELW 452

Elements, Commands & Grace

The Lutheran church celebrates two *sacraments*, or visible signs of God's grace: baptism and communion. According to Martin Luther, there are three necessary criteria for a sacrament: there must be physical elements involved, we must be commanded to do so by God in the Bible, and it must convey God's grace. In baptism, the physical element is water, which the baptismal candidate is either sprinkled with (aspersion) or immersed in, depending on tradition. (More about that in *Baptism: What We Do.*)

We hear the story of Jesus' own baptism by John the Baptist most completely in Matthew 3:13-17. John was baptizing for repentance of sins, but knew that the Messiah, Jesus, was coming, who would "baptize with the Holy Spirit." This Spirit baptism would cleanse the baptized from sins. John was very surprised when Jesus asked to be baptized, as he said, "to fulfill all righteousness." By being baptized by John, Jesus repented for the sins of the world, just as he would again on the cross, and returned humanity to a righteous relationship with God. After his resurrection, Jesus gave the disciples the Great Commission in Matthew 28:19-20, telling them to "make disciples of all nations, baptizing them" in the name of the Trinity. It is this command of Jesus we follow when we are baptized, and when we encourage others to be baptized.

There are many Bible passages about baptism in the book of Acts, about the beginning of the church. Acts 2:37-42 tells the story of the first mass baptism, when the disciples baptized 3,000 people in a day, after Peter explains that baptism is for the forgiveness of sins and giving the gifts of the Holy Spirit. Acts 8:26-40 tells the story of Philip and the Ethiopian, who after hearing the story of Jesus, replied, "Look, here is water! What is to prevent me from being baptized?" and was baptized. Just after this in chapter 9, Paul's blindness is cured when he is baptized (he is also known as Saul), and later in 16:25-34 he and Silas tell their jailer about Jesus, and he and his whole family are baptized.

1. Imagine a friend of yours had never been baptized and knew little about the Christian faith. What Bible stories or other information would you want them to know before being baptized?

Holy Spirit

In the Lutheran church we understand that faith is a gift from God, and it is God who performs all baptisms through the Holy Spirit. Therefore, we practice infant baptism, instead of insisting that a person wait until a certain age to decide to be baptized for themselves, which is believer's baptism. However, you cannot be "too old" to be baptized - if a person comes to Christianity as an older child or adult, or discovers unexpectedly that they were never baptized when they had thought they already had been, baptism is always available to them. If an older child or adult is going to be baptized, they will receive some instruction first, so they understand what baptism means and does. If an infant is baptized, their parents or guardians receive that instruction so they can teach the child as they grow.

There are two simple requirements for a person to be baptized as an adult- they must not already be baptized (there is only one baptism, and we'll talk about that more later) and that they believe that Jesus Christ, the Son of God, died and rose again to forgive their sins. The Bible is a large book and has many stories in it, and the history of the church is over 2,000 years long and contains a lot of information, but this is always the irreplaceable cornerstone. This single story is the basis of the Christian faith, and of the church which does God's work in the world.

If a person is about to die and desires to be baptized, any Christian may perform the baptism, if waiting for a worship service is not possible. The baptizer applies water to the new Christian's forehead three times, in the shape of a cross, while saying "(*Name*), I baptize you in the name of the Father, and of the Son, and of the Holy Spirit. Amen." Traditionally the person's full "Christian name," that is the first and middle names, are used. Those gathered may then pray the Lord's Prayer together. A person who has already died is not baptized, and we trust in God's infinite grace for their care.

1. Because any Christian may baptize someone who is near death, those who work in hospitals may baptize many. If you know someone who works in healthcare, ask them if they have any stories about this happening. If not, ask someone you know who's stayed in a hospital before what the experience was like, emotionally and spiritually.

One in Baptism

Since it is the Holy Spirit who baptizes, and we trust in the work of the Spirit to be fully effective, we do not have the concept of re-baptism. There are denominations which encourage those who have a revival of their faith, or who are going through a hard time in their faith, to be baptized "again." However, this implies that a baptism can wear off, or become less effective over time, and the Spirit does not work that way! A person is baptized once in the name of Trinity, as we were instructed in the Great Commission, and they remain baptized for the rest of their life. In the same way, when Christians from other denominations join the ELCA, as long as they were baptized in the name of the Father, the Son, and the Holy Spirit, their baptism is accepted and entered into our records.

Baptism should occur within a worship assembly whenever possible. Baptism is not a family event, but rather the welcoming of a new member into the Body of Christ, the church. The congregation at the baptism represents all Christians around the world, past and present, in welcoming the new Christian. Therefore, while a private or family-only baptism may, for health reasons, occasionally be necessary, baptisms are always encouraged to be held in a congregational worship setting. By practicing baptism in this way, we show by example what baptism actually means. The worshiping assembly will keep records of all baptized performed, and baptisms performed by ELCA hospital and military chaplains will be recorded by the appropriate bishop.

As we recognize only one baptism, we also acknowledge that all Christians are connected by their baptism, not only to God but to one another. While there is much discord and disunity between the various denominations and groups within Christianity, we have more unity in acknowledging one another's baptisms. Christian groups who cannot take communion with one another will often recognize one another's baptisms as valid. It is this unity in baptism which continues to encourage us to seek unity with our siblings in Christ in all churches around the world. For more on our unity in baptism, you can read Ephesians 4:1-16.

1. We often call our fellow baptized Christians our "siblings in Christ." What does that imply about what our relationships with our fellow Christians are like?

This week I will pray for:

Baptism: What We Do

Reading: Matthew 28:16-20

Hymn: I Bind Unto Myself Today ELW 450

Baptismal Promises

There are several promises made by the parents and others at a baptism of an infant. They include some promises about receiving ongoing instruction in the Christian faith, discussed below, and also 3 other promises. These are to live in community with fellow Christians, to attend worship to hear the word of God and receive communion, and to pray for and nurture the Christian life of the child. The 4 reasons for these promises are also given: so that the baptized may learn to trust God, proclaim Christ in all they do, care for God's creation, and encourage all to justice and peace. These promises are meant as a basic introduction to Christian life.

Baptism also involves some instruction. If the baptized is an infant, the parents or guardians are given some instruction which they may pass on to the child about what their baptism means. This is also often continued by the child attending Sunday School and going through a Confirmation process when they are ready to become an adult member of the congregation. There are specific promises regarding instruction made during the baptism service, including that the baptized will receive their own Bible, and be taught the

Lord's Prayer, Apostles' Creed, and 10 Commandments and what they mean (Luther's Small Catechism). Those who are baptized as adults frequently receive personal instruction from a pastor at their own pace.

Baptismal sponsors (not necessarily the same as godparents) are chosen by the baptized or their parents as guides in the Christian faith. These are people that the newly baptized can seek out with questions as they continue their Christian journey. Ideally, they should live nearby and perhaps attend the same congregation as the newly baptized. Their relationship with the newly baptized is meant to be a loving mentorship. Sometimes they are family members, but no family relationship is necessary. While the term godparents sometimes refers to baptismal sponsors as well, when referring to the parents' chosen guardians for their child if they cannot care for them, they are not always the same people.

1. There are 4 reasons listed above as the purposes of the baptismal promises- what the promises are meant to lead the baptized to do. How have these 4 purposes appeared in your life?

Daily Life in Baptism

Christians remember their baptisms each day, whenever they practice their faith. We sometimes call this "daily dying and rising," because just as Jesus died for our sins and was resurrected, we remember daily that our old sinful self has died in our baptism, and we now rise to new life in Christ. We are always both sinner and saint, broken but healed by God. No Christian is perfect, and we will continue to sin in our daily life, but in our baptism we are marked with the cross of Christ (and his sacrifice for our salvation) forever.

Ways we remember our baptism include prayer & making the sign of the cross.

A baptismal font should always be present in the worship space as a visible reminder of baptism. The font may be placed near the entrance of the sanctuary to remind worshipers of their baptisms as they enter and exit, or at the front of the sanctuary to be a visible reminder during the service. Ideally, the font should always have water in it, so that baptism is always visibly available to all who seek it. (This can sometimes be a problem- standing water left in a place for long periods of time can become contaminated or lead to mold, so this is not always possible.)

Christians often choose to intentionally remember their baptisms at times of change or upheaval in their lives, such as at the time of a major life change. Therefore, many of our worship services for life events include remembrances of our baptism, including confirmation, marriage, welcoming new members to a congregation, or the sending of missionaries. Intentional remembrance of baptism may also take place outside of the worshiping assembly, such as during the blessing of a home, while giving birth to or adopting a child, or on the occasion of retirement.

1. What are some other times in our lives when we might choose to remember our baptism? Major life events or daily events are both good ideas.

Washed in Water

There are two traditional methods of baptism, immersion and aspersion (or "sprinkling"). Immersion takes place in a pool or a large body of water, and the baptized is (carefully!) completely immersed in the water three times during the baptism. Aspersion uses a small baptismal font, and the water is poured onto the head of the baptized. Sometimes the pastor may also use a pine branch or their hands to scatter some of the baptismal water onto the assembly, as a way to remind them of their own baptisms. Both methods of baptism are equally valid and may vary depending on regional preferences, weather, or building accommodations. Whatever the method of baptism used, the baptizer is encouraged to use generous amounts of water, as a symbol of God's generosity.

Historically, congregations used to schedule most baptisms for certain days of the year, especially adult baptisms. These would be held on Pentecost, All Saints Day, the Sunday celebrating Jesus' baptism, and Easter Vigil, so that as many members of the congregation as possible could be present in support of those being baptized. Recently, as travel has become easier and families are more able to travel long distances, baptisms are more likely to be scheduled on a Sunday convenient for the family.

In addition to the baptism with water, there are certain other acts which often accompany baptism in a worship setting. The pastor may lay hands on the newly baptized and pray for the person to receive the gifts of the Holy Spirit, including faith and God's guidance. The person may be anointed with oil in the sign of the cross, as a sign that by being baptized they have entered into Jesus' death and resurrection. The person baptized may wear special clothing, often white, the color of baptism, as a sign of their status. The albs that clergy and acolytes often wear during worship services also serve as a reminder of their baptism, and are a vestige of ancient Christian churches, where all Christians wore similar white robes to worship as a sign of their faith. A candle is often presented to the newly baptized, as flame is a traditional symbol of the Holy Spirit. This candle may be lit on various occasions, such as baptismal anniversaries, to remember one's baptism.

1. Which method of baptism does your congregation usually use, immersion or aspersion? Have you ever seen a baptism of the other method?

This week I will pray for:

Church History

Early Church to the Great Schism

Reading: Matthew 16:13-20

Hymn: Built on a Rock ELW 652

After the Book of Acts

For the first few hundred years of Christianity, Christians were a tiny minority in the world, and often seen as a small group within Judaism. The Roman empire controlled the areas Christians & Jewish people lived. Other local religions were *polytheist*, worshipping more than one god. When the Romans conquered an area, the locals could keep their own gods, if they worshiped Roman gods as well. The Roman empire didn't like the Jewish people, because they refused to worship Roman gods (or any others), but they'd earned the Romans' respect through showing their long history of being *monotheists*, worshiping only one God. The Roman empire appreciated tradition, and Israel wasn't near the center of the empire, so as long as they didn't try to rebel, the Jews were allowed to remain *monotheists* and not worship Roman gods.

Christianity was spreading through the empire, including areas that had not gotten used to the idea of *monotheists*. Christians were sometimes persecuted. This was often through burning churches, but sometimes Christians were given a choice between worshiping Roman gods, or death. Many chose to be *martyrs,* those who have died because of their faith.

But some did not. Some handed over scriptures to be burned, and agreed to worship Roman gods, and even handed over other Christians in hiding to the authorities. Later on, when Christianity was more accepted, these Christians would return to the church, some as priests and even bishops. The *Donatists* believed those who fell away from the faith under persecution were not true Christians, and anything they did as a priest or bishop was not valid. They claimed any forgiveness or communion those priests or bishops offered was meaningless. *Donatism* would later be dismissed by the church as a heresy as all Christians are sinners, equal before God.

1. Do you have sympathy for those who fell away under persecution? For those who didn't want to welcome them back to the church? How would you explain your views to the other side?

Constantine

The son of a military leader, Constantine (272-337 CE) would eventually become the first sole ruler of the Roman empire in 40 years. He built the city of Constantinople (now Istanbul), changed how the Roman empire worked, and promoted Christianity throughout the world.

In a war in 312, against a rival for the throne of the empire, Constantine had a vision of a sign in the sky. The sign was the first two letters of Christ's name in the Greek alphabet: a *chi* (which looks like an X in English) overlaid by a large *rho* (which in English looks like a P), which together would be pronounced *chr.* The vision was accompanied by a voice saying, "In this sign, conquer." He had the sign painted on his and his army's armor and won the war.

The next year he and an ally would sign the Edict of Milan, which gave to all citizens the freedom to practice any religion, including Christianity. Over the rest of his life, Constantine would continue to learn about Christianity, eventually being baptized himself. Before he died, he declared Christianity the official religion of the Roman empire: people could still have other religions, but being Christian was politically helpful and got you better treatment and deals.

1. Imagine you ran a country. Would you establish an official religion? Why or why not?

Heresies and Councils

The next few centuries were full of arguments about the church and the nature of God as the church organized itself. Some of these controversies grew so heated and got so much attention that a Council would be called, and all the bishops would discuss the issue. One side of the argument would be declared *orthodox*, or correct and in keeping with Christian teachings, and the other side would be declared *heterodox*, or against Christian teachings. A *heterodox* teaching was also called a heresy. Because Christianity was now the official religion, teaching a heresy could land you in legal trouble as well as trouble with the church. The Arian Heresy, which led to the Council of Nicaea, is well known.

The Council of Nicaea was called by Constantine in 325 to discuss the teachings of a priest named Arius. Arius wanted to make it clear the church was *monotheistic*, and he could not agree with the concept of the Trinity. So, he taught that Jesus was not truly divine, just the first and most important of God's creations. The Council said that that would contradict John 1:1-15, which calls Jesus the Word of God, and that the Word *is* God, and also John 10:30, where Jesus says that he and the Father are one. Arianism was declared *heterodox*. This Council is also where the Nicene Creed comes from; the Council wrote it to help people teach how the Trinity worked.

1. Many early heresies lead to their followers being cast out of the church. Can you imagine doing that now? What would that do to the church?

The Great Schism

After Constantine, there were two cities central to the church's administration- Rome and Constantinople (now Istanbul). Constantinople administered the Eastern churches, and Rome the Western churches. Since they were so far apart, the ways they practiced their faith became different. Discord between the two cities grew. In 1054, the two sides excommunicated each other, and the church split. This was the first big split in the church until Martin Luther and the Reformation in the 1500s. In the following table, the stances shared by the Lutheran church are in *italics*. (Today Lutherans don't take a stance on icons.)

Today represented by:	Roman Catholics	Eastern Orthodox
Filioque (& from the Son) in the Nicene Creed	*Holy Spirit proceeds from the Father and the Son*	Filioque incorrect, Holy Spirit proceeds from Father only
Immaculate Conception (Mary born without sin)	Mary born without sin; no sinner could give birth to Jesus	*Mary was a normal person, & yet was chosen to mother Jesus*
Pope's Power	Pope is the head of the church	*Pope honored, but not authority*
Icons (used for prayer)	Icons are too close to idolatry	Icons help focus during prayer

1. Icons are artwork the Eastern Christians use in prayer to help them focus. Do you prefer to pray with something to focus on- a cross, a candle, etc.- or do you close your eyes?

This week I will pray for:

Reformation

Reading: Ephesians 2:1-10

Hymn: A Mighty Fortress Is Our God ELW 504

Martin Luther

Martin Luther (1483-1546) was the oldest son of working-class parents in Germany. His father wanted him to become a lawyer, which would give the family prestige and good income. He sent Martin to good schools and university, where Martin did well, and he enrolled in law school. However, on July 2, 1505, he was on his way back to school when he got caught in a terrifying thunderstorm. Convinced he was going to die on the road, far from shelter, he cried out a vow to God that if he lived, he would become a monk. He survived, and left law school to join the Augustinian monks. (He had been more interested in theology than law too, which may have also helped his decision.) His father was furious with him for "wasting" his education.

As a monk, he was a hard worker and devoted. The priest who received his confessions said Martin's confessions were some of the longest and most boring he'd ever had to listen to. However, Martin would later say that during this time he felt distant from God and doubted whether God would forgive him. His colleagues saw his gifts: two years later, he was ordained as a priest, and the next year he was sent to the University of Wittenberg. In 1512 he received his doctorate and was accepted into the faculty there, and taught classes on the Hebrew Scriptures.

1. Have you ever tried to bargain with God, or worried that you'd done something that couldn't be forgiven? How did that impact your relationship with God?

Indulgences

In 1516, Johann Tetzel arrived in Germany to sell *indulgences* for the Catholic Church, in order to fund building the new St. Peter's Basilica in Rome. An *indulgence* was a paper from the church, which declared that a person was forgiven for a certain amount of their sin and they would spend less time in Purgatory when they died. A person could receive one for themselves or another person for many reasons- services to the church, completing a pilgrimage, praying at a certain site, etc. Donating money to the church had also always been a way to receive an indulgence, as it showed commitment to the faith, but Tetzel was blatant about selling them. He was famous for the rhyme, "When a coin in the coffer rings, a soul from Purgatory springs."

Martin thought Tetzel didn't treat God's forgiveness and grace with respect. He wrote a letter to his bishop, including his *95 Theses*, a series of statements he'd written on indulgences, the church, and his worries about them, on October 31, 1517. That date is often given as the beginning of the Reformation, though he wasn't planning to separate from the Catholic Church at the time. A few months later his friends translated the *Theses* into German (he'd written them in Latin) and used a new invention- a printing press. In two weeks, copies were all over Germany, and in two months all over Europe.

1. Has anyone ever promised to forgive you for something as long as you do something special for them? Does that seem like forgiveness to you?

Diet of Worms

Martin had become convinced that God's forgiveness was more powerful than indulgences made it look. Studying the Bible, he became sure that God's forgiveness was not granted by works, such as earning an indulgence or following certain rules, but was instead granted simply as a unearned gift, through faith. He spoke out against the corruption he saw in the Church. He questioned the Pope's authority and dismissed the teaching of the Pope's infallibility *ex cathedra*: that what the Pope declared from the Throne of St. Peter in Rome was absolutely true. In 1521, Pope Leo X excommunicated him, so he could not receive communion.

But Martin did not want to leave the Catholic Church, and he wanted to fix the problems he saw. So, when the Pope demanded he present himself for further questioning and he was promised safe passage, he went. We now call this meeting the Diet of Worms. ("Diet" here means a formal assembly, and this one was held in the German city of Worms.) However, instead of discussing Luther's concerns, the Pope's representatives simply demanded he *recant*, or deny, several of his teachings. Martin said: "Unless I am convinced by the testimony of the Scriptures or by clear reason (for I do not trust either in the pope or in councils alone, since it is well known that they have often erred and contradicted themselves), I am bound by the Scriptures I have quoted and my conscience is captive to the Word of God. I cannot and will not recant anything, since it is neither safe nor right to go against conscience."

At this point, the Pope's representatives declared him to officially be a heretic. This meant it was a crime for anyone to help

Martin, and anyone could kill him and not be punished for it. However, Martin slipped out of the assembly, and on the road he was kidnapped by some men sent by Frederick, Elector of Saxony, one of Martin's greatest supporters. Frederick hid him in Wartburg Castle, and Martin spent the next year translating the New Testament into German.

1. Churches still (rarely) excommunicate, to show an unrepentant sinner how serious their sin is and encourage change. Can you imagine what might warrant this wake-up call?

Augsburg Confession

While Martin was in hiding, his friends let him know what was going on in Wittenberg. Some started encouraging changes that went beyond what Martin had planned for, which led to unrest and some riots. Several churches were vandalized or destroyed. This horrified Martin, and he returned to Wittenberg to discourage the violence. However, as Martin's teachings spread, the authority of the Catholic Church was questioned, leading to questions of other authorities. This resulted in the German Peasants' War (1524-1526), an uprising against the aristocracy. The nobility's armies put down the rebellion mercilessly, and countless thousands died.

Once the war was over, Martin settled down to organize the new church and married a former nun, Katherina von Bora. Lutherans were still not officially acknowledged by the Holy Roman Empire, who controlled Germany. The Emperor had been distracted by other concerns for years, including the Peasants' War and other possible wars. Finally, he demanded the German aristocracy declare their allegiance to the Catholic Church in 1530, at the Diet of Augsburg.

Instead, the aristocracy delivered a document called the Augsburg Confession. It contains 28 short articles, outlining the Lutheran faith. The Emperor did not have the strength to fight another war, and recognized the Lutherans, who still use the Augsburg Confession today.

1. If you had your own denomination, what would it be like? What would it focus on? How would it encourage people like you to get involved?

This week I will pray for:

Lutherans & WWII

Reading: 1 Peter 2:11-17

Hymn: By Gracious Powers ELW 626

World War II

World War II affected the German churches (Lutheran, Reformed, and others) in a way World War I hadn't: the Nazi regime took over church leadership in Germany. Because of this, World War II is an important chapter in Lutheran history. Public schools in America are forbidden from promoting any religion over another, so all students will be treated equally. Since teachers have religious preferences of their own, teaching history that involves religious conflict or ideals is very difficult. So, if you attend public school, you have learned about World War II in your history classes, but this is an aspect of that history you may not have heard. The Nazi party gained power in Germany in 1933, invaded Poland and began World War II in 1939, the United States joined the war in 1941, and the Nazis surrendered and ended that part of the war in 1945.

American churches founded by German immigrants changed in many ways during World War II. German Americans were not put into internment camps like Japanese Americans but were eager to prove their patriotism. Many churches stopped holding German-language worship services. Photos of churches in Germany, taken over by the Nazis, stunned America, as the altars in those churches had been draped with Nazi flags. German American churches reacted in two ways: some put American flags in prominent places around the church, including in the sanctuaries (but not on the altar) to show their patriotism. Others removed all national flags and symbols from church grounds, enthusiastic about the separation of church and state.

1. What if you were there, and saw those pictures of altars draped with Nazi flags? Would you want to put more American flags up in your church, or take all flags out of it? Why?

Confessing Church

Quickly after coming into power in 1933, the Nazi party encouraged the Protestant churches in Germany to join together into one national church, in order to better coordinate with the state. Many joined the new German Evangelical Church. Elections were held for church leadership, but most of the winners were not members of the Nazi party, so Hitler called for new elections, and they were rigged. Most of these rigged winners were Nazis or sympathizers and tried to remove "non-German" elements from worship, and Hebrew Scriptures from the Bible.

Soon after, the German Evangelical Church adopted the "Aryan Paragraph," which required all people in positions of power to be of "Aryan" (Northern European) descent, with no Jewish family members. So pastors and all church officials who had Jewish family or were not entirely of Northern European descent, or who were married to someone who did not fit the Aryan Paragraph, were removed from the roster. The Aryan Paragraph would also be applied to the government, schools, and many other parts of everyday life in Nazi Germany.

Many people were horrified by this, and so the Confessing Church sprang up, separate from the German Evangelical Church. It was an underground movement because being against the Aryan Paragraph meant being against the Nazi government, and that was illegal. The Confessing Church began as the Pastors' Emergency League for helping pastors of Jewish descent, headed by Martin Niemöller, who wrote: "First they came for the Socialists, and I did not speak out, because I was not a Socialist. Then they came for the Trade Unionists, and I did not speak out, because I was not a Trade Unionist. Then they came for the Jews, and I did not speak out, because I was not a Jew. Then they came for me—and there was no one left to speak for me." The Confessing Church solidified after the publication of the Barmen Declaration and remained a source of German resistance against the Nazis throughout the war.

1. The Confessing Church could not publish notices for their meetings. How would our church be different today if it was dangerous to tell anyone about it?

Barmen Declaration

The Barmen Declaration was a document written during this time, mostly by Reformed professor Karl Barth, and edited by others. It explained the reasons for the existence of the Confessing Church, and their objections to the churches under Nazi power.

These included: "We reject the false doctrine, as if the church, apart from this ministry, could give itself and allow itself to be given over to special leaders who are vested with ruling powers.... We reject the false doctrine, as if the state, beyond its special task, should and could become the single and total order of human life and thereby fulfill the intended purpose of the church. We reject the false doctrine, as if the church, beyond its special task, should and could take over state actions, state tasks, and state positions and thereby become an organ of the state."

1. What are some complications that might arise if the church ran the state? Or if the state ran the church? How would our lives be different?

Dietrich Bonhoeffer

Bonhoeffer was a German Lutheran pastor. After seminary in Germany, he went to New York City to study. While there he studied urban poverty, which led him to a lifelong thirst for justice. He liked African American spirituals and took music back to Germany with him. During this time, he changed: always fascinated by the academic study of religion, now he became passionate about his faith and the Gospel. He returned to Germany and was ordained in 1931.

Bonhoeffer was opposed to Nazism from the start and spoke out against the rigged elections of the German Evangelical church. He became a major figure in the Confessing Church and taught at their underground seminaries. He briefly returned to the United States in 1939 to teach, but regretted leaving his people behind, and returned to Germany.

Forbidden to speak in public or publish because of his opposition to the government, he took a job with the Abwehr, a military intelligence unit, and became a double agent. He was able to travel and help the German resistance and the Confessing Church. He joined a failed plot to assassinate Hitler. He realized this was attempted murder, and it weighed on him heavily, but it seemed there was no other way to stop Hitler from killing more people. In 1943 he was arrested, and moved between prisons and concentration camps, including Buchenwald, for 18 months. Finally, on April 8, 1945 he was condemned, and executed the next day. Two weeks later the camp was liberated by the Allies, and soon after the Nazis surrendered. He is still known for his books, including *The Cost of Discipleship.*

1. Bonhoeffer could have stayed in America when he came to teach in 1939. Instead he went back to try to help his country. What do you think led him to that decision?

This week I will pray for:

Slavery and the Bible

Reading: Philemon 8-21

Hymn: In Christ There Is No East Or West ELW 650

Biblical Slavery

Slavery is always a sin. Imagining a person could own another beloved child of God is horrific. And yet slavery appears all through the Bible. Characters in stories are slaves or slave-owners, there are many rules about how it worked, and it is treated as an expected aspect of society rather than a sin. Americans have a very specific image of what slavery looks like in our minds: American historical slavery that was racially based and inherited from parent to child. There are several differences between the slavery as practiced in America's history, and as in the Bible. Both are sins, but those differences do explain some of the confusion in the conversations about slavery & the Bible, before, during, and long after, the American Civil War.

There were many rules laid out in the Bible that American slavery didn't follow. First, kidnapping a person to sell them into slavery was a crime in Biblical law (Exodus 21:16). If a slave was permanently injured by their master, they were to be released to freedom in payment for the injury (Exodus 21:26-27). The Bible recognized two different kinds of slavery; foreign slaves, often prisoners of war, were usually permanently enslaved (Leviticus 25:44-46), though the above rules applied to them. An Israelite could not truly enslave another Israelite, however a person who had debts could repay them through what the Bible calls slavery, but it resembles indentured servitude. Their time of service was temporary, and afterward they would be free again (Deuteronomy 15:12-17). Finally, if a person who was a slave in another country ran away and found shelter in Israel, they could not be enslaved again or returned to their former master, they had to be provided shelter and safety (Deuteronomy 23:15-16).

We also remember that this conflict was not exactly divided between the Northern and Southern states. There were slavery advocates in New York City, and there were abolitionists in Georgia. Most Christian denominations had both abolitionists and slavery advocates as members, including the Lutherans. Some denominations split, and a small number of denominations were entirely on one side of the issue, like the Quakers. For many families in the 1800s the Bible was the only book they owned, and there were no computers. Often all people had to go on was what their pastor said or what they read in a newspaper.

1. Search the internet for "what does the Bible say about ____". Look at some of the results on the first page, how many of them look reliable? Why do you think the others are unreliable? How might you have looked into this topic in the 1800s?

One Bible, Two Conclusions

Unbelievable as it sounds, there were devout church-goers who believed Christians could be slavery advocates. Some of this was because slavery does appear in the Bible, and a few verses were used to defend the American practice of slavery. The existence of those rules, like the ones above, led many people to argue that those passages would not be in the Bible if God did not approve of slavery. There is even a passage that was put to particularly heinous use, which encouraged slaves to endure injustice (1 Peter 2:18-21). Many slave owners claimed their slaves were descendants of Ham, and therefore subject to Noah's curse (Genesis 9:20-27).

There were verses that the abolitionists found very helpful. Many talked about how God created humans in God's own image (Genesis 1:26-27), and how we could not truly love a God whose creation we enslaved. They quoted Jesus' mission to free the captive and relieve the oppressed (Luke 4:18), and Paul's claim that in Christ, all are equal, slaves or free (Galatians 3:28). Many also cited Jesus' last command to the disciples before his crucifixion, to love one another as God had loved them (John 13:34), saying that to love another person as God does could never mean enslaving them.

Yet we must admit that racism is an overwhelming force in all of this. Believing that a person should not be enslaved, and believing that a person is truly your equal, are not the same thing. Many Caucasian abolitionists, though they did much to bring about the end of slavery, still had a frankly racist view towards those who they were trying to free. The "curse of Ham" reference, cited above, was a part of this. The Union would win the Civil War, but that was not the end of the struggle. Jim Crow laws, segregation, redlining, and other racial injustices show that racism keeps us from loving one another as God has loved us and remains with us today.

1. There are some topics so close to the heart, that rational and truly open-minded Biblical study become impossible. Can you think of some subjects that you would find it dif-

ficult to discuss with someone who disagrees with you? What do those topics have in common?

The Reverend Dr. Martin Luther King, Jr.

Martin Luther King, Jr. wrote not only speeches but sermons, and he both spoke to, and prayed with, crowds. This passage is from his sermon on November 4, 1956 at Dexter Avenue Baptist Church in Montgomery, Alabama. In this sermon he uses the word *thou*. *Thou* is an word that people used to use with their family and close friends; instead of saying "you" when speaking to these special people, they would say *thou*. The title of the sermon was "Paul's Letter to American Christians," written as though the apostle Paul had written a letter to Americans at that time, and calling Sunday worship the "most segregated hour of Christian America":

"I understand that there are Christians among you who try to justify segregation on the basis of the Bible. They argue that the Negro is inferior by nature because of Noah's curse upon the children of Ham. Oh my friends, this is blasphemy. This is against everything that the Christian religion stands for. I must say to you as I have said to so many Christians before, that in Christ "there is neither Jew nor Gentile, there is neither bond nor free, there is neither male nor female, for we are all one in Christ Jesus." Moreover, I must reiterate the words that I uttered on Mars Hill: "God that made the world and all things therein . . . hath made of one blood all nations of men for to dwell on all the face of the earth."

"So, Americans I must urge you to get rid of every aspect of segregation. The broad universalism standing at the center of the gospel makes both the theory and practice of segregation morally unjustifiable. Segregation is a blatant denial of the unity which we all have in Christ. It substitutes an "I ↔ it" relationship for the "I ↔ thou" relationship. The segregator relegates the segregated to the status of a **thing** rather than elevate him to the status of a **person**. The underlying philosophy of Christianity is diametrically opposed to the underlying philosophy of segregation, and all the dialectics of the logicians cannot make them lie down together."

1. What are some examples of "I ↔ it" relationships you have in your life? What are some "I ↔ thou" relationships? How are they different? How do you act differently in them?

This week I will pray for:

ELCA History

Hymn: The Church's One Foundation ELW 654

Predecessor Bodies

When Lutherans immigrated to America in the 1700's and 1800's, they tended to form groups based on where they came from. As time went on, many of these groups joined together. By 1987, there were two large denominations who decided to join together to form the Evangelical Lutheran Church in America. They were the *American Lutheran Church* (ALC) and the *Lutheran Church in America* (LCA), and they were also joined by a smaller group, the *Association of Evangelical Lutheran Churches* (AELC).

When the ALC formed in 1960, their primary cultural background was Norwegian. They were a very *congregational* denomination in structure- each congregation did most of their own decision making, and while pastors and bishops had leadership roles, a lot of major decisions were made by laypeople. The LCA formed in 1962. Their background was largely Swedish, and their structure was *hierarchical.* Laypeople had a role in decision-making, but the bishops and pastors had more power. These differences can still be seen in congregations in the ELCA today.

The AELC was created in 1973, at an LCMS seminary in St. Louis, when a group of students and faculty staged a walkout. A few years earlier, the LCMS had elected a new leader, Pastor Jacob Preus, who refused to allow the seminary's professors to teach *historical-critical* methods of biblical interpretation, which involve learning about the time period, authors, and other works from that time; rather than only reading devotionally. The walkout protested this censorship. The group which left formed Concordia-Seminary-In-Exile, or *Seminex*, in 1974, in partnership with a now-ELCA seminary in Chicago. The AELC was formed in 1976 as those students began to graduate. There are still pastors in the ELCA who graduated from Seminex.

1. How many of your congregation's ministries and events can you list? What decisions need to be made for each? Who do you think should be responsible for those decisions?

Called to Common Mission

The ELCA has created many *full communion* agreements with other denominations. This means that the denominations agree to share pastors and communion and recognize one another's baptisms. So ELCA members are welcome to receive baptism or communion in any church of those denominations, and their members may receive in ELCA churches as well.

In 1999 the ELCA entered a full communion agreement with the Episcopal Church, "Called to Common Mission." The ELCA agreed to the *historic episcopate*, a tradition from the ancient church, when it was the bishop's duty to affirm that new pastors were orthodox, and at least 3 bishops had to attest to the orthodoxy of any new bishop, symbolized by the laying on of hands. CCM also said bishops would only give laypeople permission to preside over communion once at a time, while some bishops had given certain laypeople blanket permission.

Some members of the ELCA objected to these changes, and this lead to a split. Several congregations left the ELCA to form the LCMC, which you will learn more about in "Other Lutheran Denominations." "Called to Common Mission" is available to read online.

1. One of the reasons for the agreement was so everyone would have regular access to a fully trained pastor. Why might that regular access be a good idea?

Joint Declaration on the Doctrine of Justification

In the early 1960's, the Roman Catholic Church held a Council (similar to the Council of Nicaea, mentioned in the "Early Church to the Great Schism" lesson) to discuss modern issues facing the church. This was the Second Vatican Council, also known as Vatican II, and it led to a number of changes for the Catholic church. For example, this is when Catholic services began to be held in local languages, rather than in Latin. It was during this Council that the Pontifical Council for Promoting Christian Unity was formed, as an office of the Vatican to promote and encourage ecumenical ties with other Christians. This office began working with the Lutheran World Federation (LWF) to discuss what they had in common, and how to better work together.

In 1999, the two groups published the Joint Declaration on the Doctrine of Justification (JDDJ), which stated that the LWF and the Catholic church share a common understanding on the matter of *justification*, or how God's forgiveness works. Martin Luther's disagreement with this point of Catholic doctrine had been one reason for the Reformation. By agreeing, the LWF and the Catholic church moved a step closer towards reconciliation. In 2006, the World Methodist Conference also signed it. The document is available to read online.

1. The Catholic church and the LWF have remained in dialogue since the JDDJ. What else do you think Lutherans and Catholics might be able to agree on, or work together on?

2009 Churchwide Assembly

The 2009 Churchwide Assembly instituted a full communion agreement with the United Methodist Church, and began the Lutheran Malaria Initiative. It also adopted the Social Statement "Human Sexuality: Gift and Trust," and a set of related Recommendations. A *Social Statement* reflects on faith's impact on a social issue. It's written by a committee and voted on by the Churchwide Assembly but cannot change how the ELCA works; Recommendations do that.

The Human Sexuality Social Statement addresses several issues: marriage, divorce, dating, and so on. It emphasizes that while there are many people in the ELCA with different opinions and experiences, we can still be church together. In order to become a Social Statement, the draft had to pass with a ⅔ majority. The vote on August 19, 2009 was 676 to 338- exactly ⅔.

The Recommendations attached to the Statement included topics like developing a liturgy for families to use during a divorce, but the best known were the first two: "Resolved, that the ELCA commit itself to finding ways to allow congregations that choose to do so to recognize, support and hold publicly accountable lifelong, monogamous, same-gender relationships.... Resolved, that the

ELCA commit itself to finding a way for people in such publicly accountable, lifelong, monogamous, same-gender relationships to serve as rostered leaders of this church." They required a simple majority of over half to pass, and these did, as well as several others, including two that emphasized all people of the church respecting one another's decisions and "bound conscience." This was a callback to Martin Luther's saying he said he could not go against his own conscience at the Diet of Worms. In response, some left the ELCA to form the NALC, which you will read about in "Other Lutheran Denominations."

1. You can find the list of current Social Statements on the ELCA website, elca.org. What topics has the ELCA addressed? What topics would you want to see in the future?

This week I will pray for:

Faith Structure

ELCA Structure & Ministries

Reading: 1 Timothy 3:1-13

Hymn: We All Are One In Mission ELW 576

Congregations

The congregation is the smallest piece of the organizational structure of the ELCA. Many congregations have their own building and their own pastor (or pastors), and meet weekly for worship, but not all. Some congregations share a pastor or pastors (creating two- or three-point parishes), some meet in borrowed or rented buildings, and there are other variations. Each congregation has a constitution and a church council.

The constitution of a congregation contains the rules that it operates by, and instructions for how it's organized and governed. These are legal documents; as congregations have budgets and own buildings, there are legal requirements for how congregations need to be run. For example, because churches are exempt from paying taxes, there are certain requirements for remaining tax-exempt that the church needs to meet. Many of the rules in a constitution will have to do with the management of the congregation's money and property, and who makes decisions. Most congregations have a rule that there has to be more than one person present to count the weekly worship offering and that they can't be related to or married to each other.

The church council can be compared to a town council, it will have a President, Vice President, Treasurer, and Secretary, as well as other members. It will make decisions about the budget, ministry decisions, and the congregation's goals. The members are elected to terms of office, and rules about how many terms a person can serve in a row, or whether the whole congregation votes for the officers or just the council does, will vary from one congregation to another. The pastor or pastors of the congregation will always be members of the council. The congregation will have other committees to run specific things, such as Education or Property.

1. What committees does your congregation have? If your congregation doesn't list them on a website, you may need to look at a directory. Which groups interest you the most?

Synods

The ELCA has 65 synods, each with a bishop and staff. Synods are based on population- areas with a lot of ELCA congregations will have a lot of little synods, and areas with fewer will have a few larger synods. For example, Minnesota has 6 synods, but the Rocky Mountain Synod covers all of Colorado, New Mexico, Utah, Wyoming and part of Texas. There is also one synod that isn't geographical, the Slovak Zion Synod is a group of 30 congregations in the eastern United States who share an ethnic and cultural background.

Synods connect local congregations to each other, and to larger ministries of the church. They allow congregations to work together and help to organize charitable efforts. The bishop is the "pastor of the pastors" and also ordains new pastors, visits synod congregations and meets with other bishops to plan ministry efforts. Bishops are elected at Synod Assemblies to 6-year terms. Synod staff includes rostered leaders and non-rostered members who help congregations through all sorts of things: calling a new pastor, planning educational events, and any troubles the congregation might have.

There are two other levels of synod organization. Each synod has several conferences in it, to help local pastors get to know each other and better coordinate local ministry efforts. Also, the ELCA has 9 regions, each made up of several synods, to help organize really large-scale events.

1. Go to ELCA.org online. In the top right corner of the website click on "Find a Congregation" and find yours. Along the bottom of the box are two links, Synod and Region. Click on each one to learn more and fill in the blanks below.

I attend _____ Lutheran Church. My church is in the _____ Synod of the ELCA, in Region #_____. My synod's bishop is Bishop _____.

Churchwide

The Churchwide offices and staff are in Chicago, Illinois, at the Lutheran Center. There are several different departments at the offices, including Congregational and Synodical Mission; Global Mission; and Mission Advancement. Congregational and Synodical Mission assists with coordinating local ministry work and has resources for many kinds of ministry. Global Mission not only assists our missionaries, but also works on global disaster response, as well as international education, health, and development efforts. Mission Advancement handles communications (including the Lutheran magazine), fundraising and budgeting.

Just as a congregation has a church council, the ELCA itself also has a Church Council, which essentially is the board of directors for the denomination. The Presiding Bishop (the Churchwide-level bishop) serves as President, and there is also a Vice-President, Secretary, Treasurer, and other members, including several bishops. They meet at least twice a year.

The ELCA also has a Churchwide Assembly. They had met every other year but as of 2013 began meeting every 3 years, in various locations. The assembly is newly chosen for each meeting from the synods, with each synod sending a certain number of clergy and lay people to represent them. It is always made up of 40% clergy and 60% lay people and is about 50% women and 50% men. They vote on major decisions for the denomination, such as issuing Social Statements, deciding church policy, starting new ministries, and major budget decisions. They review the decisions of the Church Council and elect the Presiding Bishop every 6 years.

The ELCA also has a Conference of Bishops, consisting of the 65 Synodical Bishops, the Presiding Bishop, and the Secretary of the Church Council. The Conference has their own set of officers, and advise the Presiding Bishop and Church Council, especially on matters related to rostered leaders. They meet at least twice every year.

1. Go online and do a little investigating to fill in the blanks below. (Try ELCA.org and Wikipedia!)

The Presiding Bishop of the ELCA is _____, who was elected in the year _____, and before being Presiding Bishop was Bishop of the

_____ Synod. The most recent Churchwide Assembly was in the year _____ and was located in _____. The next Churchwide Assembly will be in the year _____ and will be located in _____.

This week I will pray for:

Career Ministry

Reading: 1 Corinthians 12:1-13

Hymn: Great God, Your Love Has Called Us ELW 358

Types of Professional Ministry

There are many kinds of professional ministry. All rostered leaders go through a selection process called Candidacy, which involves interviews, essays and psychological evaluations; and they all have theological training. The types of professional ministry in the ELCA are:

- **Ministry of Word and Sacrament**- Clergy of the church, also called pastors, almost always paid staff. They have a four-year college degree (in any subject) and a specialized graduate degree called a Master of Divinity, or M.Div.
  - **Specialized Calls**- these are rostered leaders who serve as chaplains (military, prison, campus, or hospital) or in interim ministry, for those between pastors.
- **Ministry of Word and Service**- Deacons are not always full-time church staff and may have various levels of ed-

ucation. They are called to many kinds of ministry in the church, including preaching, teaching, and evangelizing, but do not distribute the sacraments.

In 2016, the rosters of Associates in Ministry, Diaconal Ministers, and Deaconesses were combined into one roster of Word and Service. Deacons can work for charities or ELCA ministries, schools, or other church offices. They can work for congregations (for example, in Music Ministry or Christian Education) or do social work, or counseling. They might be a community organizer or have a day job and preach on weekends. They teach, preach, do pastoral care and any number of other ministries. More information on all of these rosters can be found on elca.org. The first step towards any rostered leadership is to contact your local synod's office.

1. A chaplain must provide care and resources for people of many different faiths. Many chaplains also work with constantly shifting groups of people. If you went into ministry, do you think you'd rather be a chaplain, a pastor in a congregation, or a deacon? Why?

Rules for Rostered Leaders

Rostered leaders in the ELCA agree to live by a document called *Definitions & Guidelines for Discipline*, which outlines rules for rostered leaders, congregations, and congregation members. All rostered leaders make promises at their ordination or consecration. They promise to accept their call to ministry from God, to teach the beliefs of the church and be a faithful witness to the Gospel, to study the Bible and be active in church, and to set an example of holy living. That part about "holy living" tends to get the most questions. Rostered leaders do not take a vow of poverty, but they do promise to be financially responsible, to support the church and charitable works, and to not seek wealth for its own sake. They also promise to be honest and trustworthy with others. They are to demonstrate compassion, justice, peacemaking, and careful stewardship of the earth, and to share the Gospel. Pastors also promise to keep private confessions confidential, unless the situation calls for mandated reporting.

There is also a section in the document about romantic relationships. All rostered leaders, if married, are to remain faithful and monogamous to their spouses. In the ELCA, if a pastor begins the process of getting divorced, or begins the process of getting remarried after a divorce, they are expected to inform their bishop, whose duty is to keep the congregation from getting hurt in the process. Rostered leaders who are not married are generally discouraged from dating within their own congregations, to keep anyone from getting hurt.

1. The inner call to ministry is a person knowing God has called them to it. The outer call is other people agreeing that the person is suited for ministry. Are both important? Why?

Married Rostered Leaders

When Martin Luther founded the Lutheran church in the 1500s, he said that pastors could be married. The Catholic church had always said that marriage was a good thing, and not less than being celibate (that is, not married). However, they did insist that priests, monks and nuns had to be celibate in order to concentrate on their calling and their work. Luther felt that having a family would allow the priest to better relate to their congregation, and that a family could be support. For the next few hundred years, in order to become a Lutheran pastor, you had to be male, never divorced, in good standing with the church, and setting a good example in your life.

Martin Luther did not allow for the orders of monks and nuns from the Catholic church to continue in the new Lutheran church. Over time many Protestant churches realized that many people have a call to ministry that does not involve being a pastor, and groups of Word and Service ministers have grown. Lutherans have often had strong Deaconess programs.

1. What traits or qualities are most important to you in a religious leader? Why do these matter to you? Do you think other people you know would have a different list?

Diverse Rostered Leaders

Within the last hundred years, some denominations have begun allowing divorced people to become pastors, and for pastors who divorce to remain on the roster and in ministry. The idea behind this is that pastors are not perfect, and they and their family members cannot be expected to be perfect. Sometimes the best choice for those involved involves divorce, and if all pastors who get divorced also lose their jobs, that puts unhealthy pressure on pastors and their families.

More recently, some denominations have begun ordaining women. Many of the reasons that women had not been allowed into professional ministry were based on traditions and culture. However, Christianity has often gone against what culture would do. The Bible does have a few verses against women being in church leadership, but the larger context makes it clear those are culture-based. There are also several women in the Bible who have visible roles of church leadership. The denominations that became the ELCA started ordaining women in the 1970s.

In 2009, the ELCA's Churchwide Assembly voted to ordain people who were in same-gender lifelong publicly-accountable monogamous relationships. As same-gender marriage was not legal in all states, the assembly did not require legal marriage, but all other requirements for these couples were the same as the expectations for those who were legally married.

1. Many people have said that having a pastor who shared major characteristics with them was a powerful experience. Why do you think this would matter?

This week I will pray for:

Other Lutheran Denominations

Reading: Galatians 3:23-4:7

Hymn: Out Of The Depths I Cry To You ELW 600

Lutheran Church - Missouri Synod (LCMS)

Basics: The LCMS was founded in 1847 but went through many changes to reach its current structure in 1947. The LCMS originally hails from a group of German immigrants to America who settled in Missouri in the late 1830's. About half of the denomination's members are in the Upper Midwest, but they are spread throughout the USA. They have been well known for their system of private schools. Their headquarters are in Kirkwood, Missouri, and they are the 2nd largest Lutheran denomination in the USA.

What We Share: Besides the Christian basics (belief in Jesus' resurrection, the creeds, the sacraments, reading the Bible) the LCMS are guided by the Book of Concord. Like the ELCA, they read the Bible through the lens of Christ, and teach that Christ is truly present in, with and under the bread and wine at communion. They reject the idea of the "Rapture" (as do all other Lutheran denominations listed here), and their confirmation process is very strong on education.

How We're Different: The LCMS does not ordain women as pastors, though women can vote in their congregational meetings and be on councils. They do not allow communion until after they have been confirmed, and practice *closed table* communion: only baptized and confirmed members of the LCMS may receive communion at their churches. They avoid most *ecumenical* (that is, with other Christian denominations) ties, though they do a lot of work with Lutheran World Relief, a global aid organization that the ELCA also works with. Their pastors and members may participate in certain types of public ecumenical worship, but they do not share pastors with other denominations in the USA. The LCMS also teaches biblical inerrancy and six-day creationism and does not allow same-gender marriage.

1. Think about the differences between *closed table* communion, and *open table* communion (all Christians welcome). What do each say to members? To visitors?

Wisconsin Evangelical Lutheran Church (WELS)

Basics: The WELS was founded in 1850, and came from a similar background as the LCMS. The two used to be in fellowship together (sharing communion and pastors, and so on) but broke off in 1961 because the LCMS was in conversation with another Lutheran denomination (which later became part of the ELCA) and the WELS did not approve. They are a smaller denomination than the LCMS and are headquartered in Milwaukee, Wisconsin.

What We Share: The ELCA shares with the WELS all that it shares with the LCMS. There are several differences between the WELS and the LCMS, however. The WELS are in full fellowship with the Evangelical Lutheran Synod, or ELS, in Minnesota, and with them have a global ministry fellowship called the Confessional Evangelical Lutheran Conference, or CLEC.

How We're Different: The WELS does not ordain women or allow them to have any authority over men, so they cannot vote or be on councils that would make decisions for any of the men. They emphasize the traditional European worship style, and rarely venture into contemporary or multicultural worship styles. They practice *closed table* communion and require members to be confirmed before taking communion. Before they are willing to engage in any ecumenical ties, they require full agreement on all matters of doctrine. Members cannot participate in ecumenical prayers or services. They teach six-day Creationism and Biblical inerrancy, and do not allow same-gender marriage.

1. The WELS church only works with denominations it agrees with completely. What do you think we need to agree on to work together? To share pastors and communion?

Lutheran Congregations in Mission for Christ (LCMC)

Basics: LCMC began in 2001, primarily from congregations breaking off from the ELCA. In 1999, the ELCA entered a full communion agreement with the Episcopal Church. This agreement was settled in a document called *Called to Common Mission* or CCM, which is discussed at more length in the ELCA History lesson. The ELCA agreed to something which some congregations disagreed with, and the LCMC was formed two years later. LCMC is the next smallest Lutheran denomination in the US after WELS.

What We Share: The LCMC and the ELCA have a lot in common, as the split was fairly recent. They do ordain women and teach the Book of Concord. They practice the sacraments the same way that the ELCA does, though they are not in full communion with the ELCA.

How We're Different: They do not have a hierarchy like the ELCA does (pastor, bishop, presiding bishop) or synods. Instead, congregations write their own policies and constitutions, call pastors without oversight, and are almost completely independent. They have two boards, and some coordinators who help congregations stay in touch and suggest resources, but they do not have power over the congregations. They also do not allow same-gender marriage.

1. The LCMC lets each congregation decide almost everything for themselves. Can you see the strengths of this system? The weaknesses?

North American Lutheran Church (NALC)

Basics: The NALC was founded in 2010 in Ohio, and their current central office is in Hilliard, Ohio. They were founded by a group of congregations (called Lutheran CORE or Lutheran Coalition for Renewal) who left the ELCA after Churchwide Assembly in 2009 when the ELCA chose to ordain those who were in same-gender marriages. They have an agreement to share pastors with the Anglican Church in North America (not the Episcopal Church) and are seeking relationships with other denominations as well.

What We Share: The NALC and the ELCA share many things, because the split was so recent. The NALC has congregations with a variety of worship styles, and they teach the Book of Concord as well as standard Christian subjects such as Bible study and regular prayer. They have a similar hierarchy. They ordain women and women may hold any leadership role in the church.

How We're Different: Partly because of their size, they just have one bishop. They have fewer ecumenical relationships and fewer staff and ministries. They very strongly discourage their pastors from divorce- a pastor in a call who gets divorced can be removed from the leadership roster, except in special circumstances. The ELCA and NALC are not in full communion. They do not allow same-gender marriage.

1. Leaving a denomination can be very painful. What might make you consider it?

This week I will pray for:

Other Christian Denominations

Reading: 1 Corinthians 12: 12-26

Hymn: We All Believe In One True God ELW 411

Roman Catholic Church (RCC)

History: The Roman Catholic Church, one of the oldest religious groups in the world with about one billion members, is a global organization. The RCC (which doesn't consider itself a denomination) has had a huge impact on world history. It has not only been a spiritual authority in the world, but for hundreds of years has also been a political force. Knowing the history of the Catholic Church can helpful for two reasons: many of the problems the RCC has faced still pop up in various denominations; and the ripples of those controversies still affect the world.

Beliefs: The RCC has a different understanding from Lutherans of what a sacrament is, so they have 7 sacraments, whereas Lutherans have 2. The Catholic Church also grants Mary, the mother of Jesus, a special role: she is seen as an advocate with God for people, especially as a figure who can be asked to encourage God to grant grace to sinners. They practice closed table communion, and have various traditions that Lutherans do not share, such as a meat fast on Fridays during Lent. The worship services (Mass) do not vary much between congregations.

Organization: The Roman Catholic Church has a strong sense of hierarchy. The denomination is lead by the Bishop of Rome, or the Pope, followed by Bishops, Priests, and Deacons. Priests must be male and celibate. The religious orders include men and women who have decided to devote their lives to their religious calling: they might be *cloistered,* living apart from the world, or not. The most recent major changes to the denomination happened due to a Council commonly called Vatican II in the 1960s. This Council allowed congregations to hold worship services in the local languages, instead of in Latin, among other changes.

1. How might being global affect how the RCC reacts to major world events or issues?

United Methodist Church (UMC)

History: The Methodist movement was founded in England by the Wesley brothers, John and Charles, in the 1700s. Charles Wesley is also known for his many well-loved hymns including *Hark the Herald Angels Sing,* and *Jesus Christ is Risen Today.* They were both ministers in the Church of England (known as the Episcopal Church in America) and neither wanted to leave it, though the movement would eventually do so after their deaths. They sought to reform the Anglican Church in certain ways. Methodist churches played a large role in the Temperance movement and the Prohibition laws in America and are against gambling.

Beliefs: Methodists see Holy Communion as more of a memorial of the Last Supper and Crucifixion, rather than believing that Christ is truly present "in, with and under" the elements as Lutherans put it. They do consider both Baptism and Communion to be sacraments, and their worship service styles vary quite a bit. The Methodist movement emphasizes social justice work, lively worship services, and the idea that it is possible to achieve "Christian perfection" in life. The ELCA and United Methodist Church are in full communion with each other.

Organization: The denomination is global, and not based in any one country. Methodist ministers are *itinerant*, which means that they do not choose their congregations, but ministers are assigned, and often moved every 3 years. They have Bishops, and Conferences and Districts.

1. Methodists believe that "Christian perfection" is possible. Do you believe that a person can achieve "Christian perfection"? For a moment, or a month, or a lifetime?

Presbyterian Church USA (PCUSA)

History: John Calvin, who broke away from the Roman Catholic Church in 1530 (a decade after Luther) became a great reformer of the church. In America, the denomination he founded is now called the Reformed Church. Calvin put a lot of work into the organization and structure of the church and is still famous for his *Institutes of the Christian Religion*, a shelf-full of books on God, the Bible, and the church. One of Calvin's students, John Knox, traveled to Scotland and founded the Presbyterian denomination. Knox was also involved in political upheaval there with Mary, Queen of Scots.

Beliefs: Presbyterians have the Five Points of Calvinism, often referred to as TULIP. TULIP stands for *Total depravity* (everyone is a sinner); *Unconditional election* (God's grace is a gift with no conditions to those God chooses); *Limited atonement* (Christ's death on the cross was only for those God chooses to save); *Irresistible grace*

(God's grace is not something that can be resisted); and *Perseverance of the saints* (salvation is not something that can be lost).

Organization: The Presbyterians refer to their structural organization as their *polity*. Elders lead worship and provide pastoral care, but their main focus is often on teaching the faith. A church council is called a *session*. Congregations are part of a local *presbytery* as Lutherans belong to a synod, but presbyteries have different types of authority over their congregations than Lutheran synods do. The presbyteries are organized into synods which are more like ELCA regions and cover a wide area. The national General Assembly meets every two years.

1. Lutherans agree with some points of TULIP and disagree with others. Which seem to match up with what you've heard in church? Which do not?

American Baptist Churches USA (ABCUSA)/Southern Baptist Convention (SBC)

History: Long before the American Civil War, many Baptist churches in the US belonged to what is now called American Baptist Churches USA. In 1845, they voted to not allow people who owned slaves to be ordained as missionaries, and many congregations where slavery was still legal, left the denomination to form the Southern Baptist Convention. The SBC would slowly come to the position of racial equality, working particularly hard since the 1940s to become more diverse. They elected their first African American president in 2012.

Beliefs: Baptists practice communion similarly to the Methodists. Instead of *infant baptism*, all those who are to be baptized must be old enough to understand what it means, often called *believer's bap-*

tism. This age varies, but often is at least 6 or 7 years old. While Baptists do accept the Apostles' & Nicene Creeds, they prefer members to state their faith in their own words.

Organization: The Baptist tradition has a history of congregations being very independent. Many modern Baptist congregations do not actually belong to any denomination, preferring to be entirely independent. The ABCUSA ordains women and has a strong relationship with the United Church of Christ (UCC). The SBC does not ordain women.

1. What does infant baptism say about God's role in our lives? Believer's baptism?

This week I will pray for:

Other Religions

Reading: Luke 10:25-37

Hymn: This Is My Song ELW 887

Judaism

History: Jesus was Jewish, but the way Jesus practiced Judaism 2,000 years ago was very different than how it is practiced today. The Jewish Temple, destroyed in 70 CE, has never been rebuilt, and today Judaism is synagogue-focused rather than Temple-based. One of the best-known Jewish theologians is Rabbi Moshe ben Maimon, also known as Rambam or Maimonides. He was a medieval-era Rabbi who was gifted at explaining theological ideas in an understandable manner. Jews have often faced persecution, and antisemitism is still active in the world today. Partly because of this, being Jewish is not only a religious identity but also an ethnic or cultural identity - there are people who identify themselves as Jewish atheists.

Beliefs: A central verse of Scripture for Judaism is Deuteronomy 6:4, also known as the *Shema*: "Hear, O Israel; the LORD our God, the LORD is one." Aside from having one God, Judaism varies in beliefs as much as Christianity does. Rambam came up with a list of 13 basic beliefs, including that the dead will be resurrected. However not all of them are universally accepted, for example the

Sadducees in the Bible didn't believe in resurrection. Many Jewish people regard Jesus as a gifted teacher, but they don't believe Jesus was the Messiah, or divine.

Organization: There are three main branches of Judaism today: Orthodox, Conservative, and Reformed. One of the best known current Jewish faith practices is keeping kosher, which involves the separation of meat and dairy products for meals, and various other rules; but not all Jewish people keep kosher. Another practice is using "G-d" instead of "God" when writing, to avoid using God's name lightly. There are currently about 14 million Jews scattered around the world, and the term *diaspora* refers to Jewish people who live outside modern-day Israel, which was established in 1948, after WWII.

1. Read Deuteronomy 6:1-9. Who is speaking in these verses? What instructions are the Jewish people given? What does the narrator seem to want for the Jewish people?

Islam

History: The followers of the faith of Islam are called Muslims. The founder of Islam was Muhammad, known as the last prophet sent by God (after Abraham, Moses, Jesus, and others). In 610 CE he began having a series of revelations from God, which he wrote down over the years into what would become the Qur'an. The Islamic faith came to be centered in Mecca, which is now in Saudi Arabia. There are two major groups within Islam, the Sunni and the Shia. The original split between the groups, less than 100 years after Muhammad's death, was over disputes about who should lead Islam - the *caliph*. Sunnis wanted elections, and the Shia believed that relatives of Muhammad should lead. Today, Sunnis are the majority, at least ¾ of Muslims today. There are about 1.5 billion Muslims, and Islam the second largest religion in the world next to Christianity. The country with the largest Muslim population is Indonesia.

Beliefs: Islam and Judaism agree on the centrality of God being one and being the only God. They reject the Christian concept of the Trinity on those grounds (though Christians also understand themselves to be *monotheists*, just as Muslims and Jews are). The Five Pillars of Islam, necessary beliefs and practices for Muslims, are shared by both Sunni and Shia, though their precise interpretations are slightly different. The Five Pillars include a statement of belief that God is the only God and Muhammad is God's messenger (the *Shahadah*); prayer five times per day; giving 2.5% or more of one's wealth to the poor; following the fast of the month of Ramadan as medically possible; and pilgrimaging to Mecca if possible (the *Hajj*). Muslims believe Jesus was an important prophet, but not divine or the Son of God.

Organization: The two denominations have many differences in religious practice and ethics by now, but both agree on the centrality of Muhammad's role as prophet and the accuracy of the Qur'an. Also, while there are many modern translations of the Qur'an into various languages for study purposes, both denominations agree that the Qur'an can only be truly understood in the original language of Arabic. All Muslims who are not native speakers of Arabic will at least take a few Arabic classes, and many seek fluency.

1. Complete this analogy: terrorists who claim to act in the name of Islam are to Islam, as ____ are to Christianity. How do you feel about these Christian extremists?

Buddhism

History: Siddhartha Gautama was born in what is now India, in the 5th century BCE. His father was the leader of the area. When he was 29 Siddhartha left his family home on a spiritual quest to learn from area teachers. He experimented with *asceticism* (practice of extreme simplicity), especially fasting, but eventually came to a practice of moderation, or the "Middle Way": moderate simplicity. (For example, having small and simple meals, but not fasting entirely.) At 35 he famously sat beneath a fig tree with the goal of achieving complete enlightenment. According to his disciples, he rose several days later having become the first person to completely liberate himself from the cycle of *Samsara*, worldly concerns one faces in reincarnations. His title, Buddha, is recognition of this achievement of *Nirvana*.

Beliefs: Buddhism is a *nontheistic* religion, which means that the religion does not involve belief in a deity. Instead, Buddhism is a way of life based on teachings from the Buddha, especially the Noble Eightfold Path, or the Middle Way: right view, right intention, right speech, right action, right livelihood, right effort, right mindfulness, and right concentration. These and the other Buddhist teachings make up *dharma*, or teachings that a Buddhist person follows. The goal is to leave the cycle of reincarnation - being born over and over again - by achieving enlightenment and ending one's suffering, which is the focus of the Middle Way. In order to do this one tries to live "gently," making minimal negative impact on the world. Buddhist practices include pacifism, mindfulness, meditation, and yoga, though certainly all of those can also be practiced by non-Buddhists to an extent. Buddhism also has a strong *monastic* tradition.

Organization: There are a number of Buddhist groups, usually known as schools rather than denominations. Two of the major schools are *Theravada* and *Mahayana*. Theravada Buddhism is centered in Sri Lanka and Southeast Asia. This school understands enlightenment to be a sudden moment of insight. Mahayana Buddhism is centered in India, and also includes Zen and Tibetan Buddhism and other smaller traditions. This school sees enlightenment as an ongoing process, with several possible methods of achieving it. Buddhism is not as doctrinal as many other world religions are - there are many ways to follow Buddhism.

1. Many non-Buddhists borrow Buddhist practices, like yoga. How can we do so respectfully?

This week I will pray for:

Church Calendar

Season of Pentecost Holidays

Reading: Acts 2:1-14, 22-24, 37-42

Hymn: Come, Join the Dance of Trinity ELW 412

Pentecost Sunday

When is it? Pentecost is the Sunday that finishes the season of Easter; we celebrate it about 50 days after Easter Sunday. The name _Pentecost_ is the Greek word for the Jewish holiday that is called _Shavuot_ (_shah-voo-oht_), or the Festival of Weeks. Shavuot happens 50 days after Passover, and celebrates God giving the Torah to Moses. The British call Pentecost Whitsunday.

What is it about? We celebrate Pentecost as the anniversary of the story in Acts 2, when the Holy Spirit descended on the apostles and gave them the gift of speaking many languages. After the Holy Spirit came to them, they began to act strangely, and crowds gathered to watch them, confused. Peter gave a sermon explaining what had happened to them, and 3,000 people became Christians and were baptized that day. Pentecost is sometimes called the Birthday of the Church.

How do we celebrate it? Because Pentecost is about the arrival of the Holy Spirit, we surround ourselves with images of the Holy Spirit: the color red reminds us of the "tongues of flame" that touched the disciples; pictures of doves (as the Holy Spirit appeared at Jesus' baptism); wind and water, for the great rushing wind in the Pentecost story and for baptism. It's a joyful Sunday, a celebration as we remember God is active in the world. Many people wear red for Pentecost.

What other ways do people celebrate Pentecost? Many churches have services in multiple languages on this day, or at least have the Lord's Prayer spoken in many languages. This is a popular day to have baptisms, and many churches have their confirmation services on this day. Historically, this is a day for great feasts. In England it's traditional to have parades, where the children of the congregation dress in white and, together with the pastor, walk through town.

1. We often speak differently around our friends than we do with our family, or at church. What are some different "languages" you speak? Could the Holy Spirit speak through you in these languages?

Holy Trinity Sunday

When is it? Holy Trinity Sunday is the first Sunday after Pentecost. It's the first Sunday in "Ordinary Time," the long church season after Pentecost. During Ordinary Time there aren't many holidays, and the color of the season is green. This season continues until Advent begins. However, to make it obvious this is a special day, the color for Holy Trinity is white.

What is it about? The early church realized that the Trinity was a difficult idea for a lot of people. The idea of a Triune God, the Three-in-One, is confusing to many Christians, so a Sunday was devoted to it in order to better explain the idea. This day moved around the church calendar in the early church, but finally became the Sunday after Pentecost in the early 1900s.

How do we celebrate it? On many Sundays we concentrate on one person of the Trinity. On Pentecost we focus on the Holy Spirit, on Christmas and Easter we focus on Jesus, and there are many Sundays in Ordinary Time that focus on Creation and God the Father. This Sunday we celebrate all three persons of the Trinity and try to explain how it works.

What other ways do people celebrate Holy Trinity? Many churches recite the Athanasian Creed on this Sunday. You've read the Apostle's Creed and the Nicene Creed: the Athanasian Creed is much longer and spells out how the Trinity works in much more detail.

1. Read through the Athanasian Creed. What surprises you? Does anything in it concern you? Do you think there are any reasons besides the length and old-fashioned language that we don't read this every Sunday?

All Saints Sunday

When is it? All Saints Sunday and All Saints Day are not always the same day- like when a holiday lands on a weekend, so we "observe" it on a Friday or Monday so people can have time off work. All Saints Day is the day after Halloween, November 1. However, since Lutherans celebrate Reformation Day on the Sunday nearest to October 31, they are always celebrated in a row, Reformation Sunday one week and All Saints Sunday the next.

What is it about? All Saints Day is connected to Halloween! Hundreds of years ago, when Halloween was called All Hallows Eve, the day was thought to be a time when the "wall" between the worlds of the living and of the dead thinned, and "the dead would walk" that evening. All the traditions about costumes and treats and tricks came out of that. The next morning, as soon as the night was over, everyone would go to church and pray for all those who had died- Christians on November 1, and everyone else on November 2 ("All Souls Day").

How do we celebrate it? In the Lutheran church we do not pray for the dead- they are with God and need nothing. However, in on All Saints Sunday we remember and give thanks for the lives of the members of the congregation who have died over the year, and others, especially Christians who have helped to shape our faith. We light candles in remembrance and pray for those in mourning.

What other ways do people celebrate All Saints? In some countries, children go around asking for candy on All Saints instead of on Halloween. This is also a day when Christians around the world will go to the graves of their relatives and leave flowers. In Mexico, the "Day of the Dead" spans three days, October 31 to November 2, and has a lot of traditions of its own.

1. Ask an adult for stories about people who they give thanks for on All Saints Sunday. Who has taught them what it means to be a Christian? How did they do that teaching?

This week I will pray for:

Athanasian Creed

Whoever desires to be saved should above all hold to the catholic faith. Anyone who does not keep it whole and unbroken will doubtless perish eternally.

Now this is the catholic faith:

That we worship one God in trinity and the trinity in unity, neither blending their persons nor dividing their essence.

For the person of the Father is a distinct person, the person of the Son is another, and that of the Holy Spirit still another.

But the divinity of the Father, Son, and Holy Spirit is one, their glory equal, their majesty coeternal.

What quality the Father has, the Son has, and the Holy Spirit has.

The Father is uncreated, the Son is uncreated, the Holy Spirit is uncreated.

The Father is immeasurable, the Son is immeasurable, the Holy Spirit is immeasurable.

The Father is eternal, the Son is eternal, the Holy Spirit is eternal.

And yet there are not three eternal beings; there is but one eternal being.

So too there are not three uncreated or immeasurable beings; there is but one uncreated and immeasurable being.

Similarly, the Father is almighty, the Son is almighty, the Holy Spirit is almighty.

Yet there are not three almighty beings; there is but one almighty being.

Thus the Father is God, the Son is God, the Holy Spirit is God.

Yet there are not three gods; there is but one God.

Thus the Father is Lord, the Son is Lord, the Holy Spirit is Lord.

Yet there are not three lords; there is but one Lord.

Just as Christian truth compels us to confess each person individually as both God and Lord, so catholic religion forbids us to say that there are three gods or lords.

The Father was neither made nor created nor begotten from anyone.

The Son was neither made nor created; he was begotten from the Father alone.

The Holy Spirit was neither made nor created nor begotten; he proceeds from the Father and the Son.

Accordingly, there is one Father, not three fathers; there is one Son, not three sons; there is one Holy Spirit, not three holy spirits.

Nothing in this trinity is before or after, nothing is greater or smaller; in their entirety, the three persons are coeternal and co-equal with each other.

So in everything, as was said earlier, we must worship their trinity in their unity and their unity in their trinity.

Anyone then who desires to be saved should think thus about the trinity.

But it is necessary for eternal salvation that one also believes in the incarnation of our Lord Jesus Christ faithfully.

Now this is the true faith:

That we believe and confess that our Lord Jesus Christ, God's Son, is both God and human, equally.

He is God from the essence of the Father, begotten before time; and he is human from the essence of his mother, born in time; completely God, completely human, with a rational soul and human flesh; equal to the Father as regards divinity, less than the Father as regards humanity.

Although he is God and human, yet Christ is not two, but one.

He is one, however, not by his divinity being turned into flesh, but by God's taking humanity to himself.

He is one, certainly not by the blending of his essence, but by the unity of his person.

For just as one human is both rational soul and flesh, so too the one Christ is both God and human.

He suffered for our salvation; he descended to hell; he arose from the dead; he ascended to heaven; he is seated at the Father's right hand; from there he will come to judge the living and the dead.

At his coming, all people will arise bodily and give an accounting of their own deeds.

Those who have done good will enter eternal life, and those who have done evil will enter eternal fire.

This is the catholic faith: one cannot be saved without believing it firmly and faithfully.

Seasons Related to Christmas

Reading: Matthew 2:7-23

Hymn: O Come, O Come, Emmanuel ELW 257

Advent

When is it? There are 4 Sundays of the season of Advent, which is the season before Christmas. If Christmas Day lands on a Monday, that means that the fourth Sunday of Advent will be on Christmas Eve. The color of the season is blue, because in traditional Christian artwork, Mary, Jesus' mother, was often shown wearing blue. There are many theories about why; one is that the Ark of the Covenant in the Old Testament was always covered in blue cloth, so Mary wearing blue shows that God is present with her, just as God was present with the Ark.

What is it about? Advent is the season of waiting for Christmas, in the same way that Lent is the season of waiting for Easter. Advent is also the first season of the church year- so the "New Year's Day" of the church calendar is the first Sunday of Advent.

How do we celebrate it? During Advent, we read stories from the Bible that prepare us for Jesus' arrival, and we sing Advent hymns. Many churches, and some people's homes, have an Advent wreath with four candles around the outside and one in the middle. Each candle is lit on each Sunday in Advent, and the center candle (the Christ candle) is lit on Christmas Day. Some families might have an Advent calendar, which is a newer tradition and not always religious.

What stories do we read from the Bible? On the first Sunday of Advent, we read about Jesus prophesying his return- often called the Second Coming. This reminds us that we're in a sort-of Advent today. The middle two Sundays are readings on John the Baptist's ministry and prophecy of Jesus' arrival. The fourth Sunday of Advent is about the coming of Jesus' birth.

1. During Advent, we remember Jesus was truly human. What kind of teen do you think Jesus was? Who would he have been friends with? What would he have cared about?

Christmas

When is it? Christmas Day is celebrated on December 25, and in recent years Christmas Eve has become important as well. We don't know the exact date of Jesus' birth, so the early church chose this date to coincide with winter solstice celebrations, which were already common. Historians have recently realized that our count of the years since Christ's birth is off, and Jesus was probably born sometime between 7 and 2 BCE. The church season of Christmas lasts through January 5. The colors for the season of Christmas are white and gold, just like Easter.

What is it about? Christmas is short for "Christ's Mass"- or the mass (communion service) celebrating Christ's birth. This is not just a "birthday party" for Jesus, because it's also about our slow realization each year that God, who is all-powerful, was willing to come to earth and be a human being, to live and to die among us. This is called the *Incarnation*, which means "becoming human," but when it's capitalized it refers to Jesus as God Incarnate.

How do we celebrate it? Christmas carols are a common way of celebrating Christmas. The practices of having a good meal, and having many candles lit around the house, is also very old. Christmas presents are a more recent invention, in the last few hundred years; and Christmas cards are perhaps a century old. Christmas trees were a German tradition that became better known when Queen Victoria of England started having them at her castles, because her husband was German. Stories of Santa Claus were adapted from traditions of St. Nicholas, the saint of children, who went around the world giving small treats to children on his saint's day, December 6. Many Swedish churches have had a *Julotta*, which is a sunrise Christmas Day service. Some churches have started a "Blue Christmas" service, which is for people who find the holiday season difficult, especially those who are grieving. Christmon trees, decorated with religious symbols, are a new tradition. Many non-religious "traditions" have sprung up recently as well.

What stories do we read from the Bible? On Christmas we usually read either the story of the birth of Christ in Luke 2, or we read John 1:1-14, which is about what Christ's birth meant.

1. Our Christmas gift from God didn't cost any money. What are some gifts of time, service, or thoughtfulness you could give to those you love?

Epiphany

When is it? The Day of Epiphany is January 6 and is often celebrated on the Sunday after New Year's. The Sunday after that is the Baptism of Our Lord. The color of the day for both these days is white. The season of Epiphany is 6 to 8 weeks long, and during these Sundays the color is green. The season of Epiphany lasts until Lent begins. The last Sunday of the season is Transfiguration, and its color is white.

What is it about? The day of Epiphany, the twelfth day of Christmas (as in the song "The Twelve Days of Christmas") has also been called Twelfth Night. It is the beginning of the season of Epiphany, which is the only church season named after what *we're* doing. We, the people of the church, are having an epiphany about what Jesus' birth means for the world. A major theme of the season of Epiphany is light, referring to Jesus as "the light of the world" as in the first chapter of John. The season of Epiphany also includes our celebrations of Jesus' baptism and of the Transfiguration, which was the disciples witnessing that Jesus was truly divine on a mountaintop.

How do we celebrate it? Twelfth Night has many traditions, including a special "king's cake," and feasting. In medieval England it was celebrated as a day when the nobility would serve the servants and the servants would have their own party, the "Day of Misrule."

What stories do we read from the Bible? On Epiphany we read the story of the visit of the three wise men to the infant Jesus, in Matthew 2. On the Baptism of Our Lord we read the story of Jesus' baptism in Gospels. On Transfiguration Sunday we read the story of the Transfiguration.

1. Epiphany has been celebrated as a day when all the usual power structures are turned upside down, like how God became a tiny infant. Who does most of the work in your house? Who gets most of the benefits of that work? What would change if you had a Day of Misrule at home?

This week I will pray for:

Seasons Related to Easter

Reading: John 20:19-29
Hymn: Now All the Vault of Heaven Resounds ELW 367

Lent

When is it? Lent is the season before the Three Days and Easter, and it lasts for 6 weeks, from Ash Wednesday to the day before Maundy Thursday. The Sundays during Lent are "days off" from the rigors of Lent, or "little Easters" as Luther called them. After subtracting the Sundays, Lent is 40 days long- which lines up with the 40 days Jesus spent being tempted by Satan, and the 40 years that Moses lead Israel through the wilderness after leaving Egypt. The color for Lent is purple, a color of royalty. Some change the color on Palm Sunday to scarlet, for Jesus' blood.

What is it about? Lent is a time of self-examination, repentance, and simplification. We spend this time slowly coming to recognize that in order to get to Easter morning, we first go through Good Friday and the rest of the Three Days. During Lent we try to understand what that means.

How do we commemorate it? On Ash Wednesday, we have the longest, most detailed confession of the church year- and there is no forgiveness offered yet. While the Sunday services during Lent will have Confession and Forgiveness as usual, this is a confession that we stay in through the whole season of Lent. At this point we also receive ashes on our forehead, acknowledging our mortality. During the season of Lent, we do not sing "Alleluia" during worship services, and services are more solemn than they are during other times of the year. Traditionally those desiring baptism during Lent were encouraged to wait until Holy Saturday, but this is less common now. The final Sunday of Lent is Palm Sunday, which celebrates Jesus' triumphal entry into Jerusalem, but towards the end of the service we realize what is about to happen.

What stories do we read from the Bible? The Gospel stories that we read during Lent begin with Jesus revealing to his disciples he will die, and then they journey towards Jerusalem & the cross.

1. For Lent some people give up either a luxury, or a bad habit hurting their relationship with God and/or others, and instead focus on Bible study, prayer, and giving to charity. What are some bad habits people might choose to give up for Lent, that hurt a person's relationship with God or with other people? DO NOT NAME NAMES.

Three Days

When is it? The Three Days are between Lent and Easter, and are technically their own, very short, church season: Maundy Thursday, Good Friday, and Holy Saturday. Maundy Thursday is the same color as Palm Sunday. Good Friday has no color because the sanctuary is stripped.

What is it about? Maundy Thursday is the commemoration of the Last Supper, including the first Holy Communion, Jesus washing the disciples' feet, and Jesus giving his final commandment: "Love one another as I have loved you." The word "Maundy" comes from the Latin word for "commandment". Good Friday commemorates Jesus Christ's crucifixion and death and is the most solemn day of the church year. Holy Saturday, or the Easter Vigil, begins as a deathwatch, but at the very end of the service, the tomb is found empty, to the congregation's amazement. The actual resurrection is never a part of Holy Saturday, it ends with the tomb being empty.

How do we commemorate it? The service on Maundy Thursday begins with a forgiveness of sins that reminds us of the confession we made on Ash Wednesday. Maundy Thursday services always include communion. There may also be a foot washing part of the service, or a reenactment of the Last Supper. The service ends with stripping the altar, in preparation for Good Friday. Good Friday services include prayers for all people of the world, including non-Christians, and acknowledgement of the cross. Easter Vigil services are less common, but involve the lighting of a new Paschal Candle, several Bible readings outlining the Hebrew Scriptures, and baptisms put on hold during Lent are celebrated.

What stories do we read from the Bible? On Maundy Thursday, we read the story of the Last Supper, and on Good Friday, we read the story of Jesus' crucifixion and death. Holy Saturday readings are more extensive, an overview of the Hebrew Scriptures and finding the empty tomb.

1. Imagine a Christian who does not attend church very often, but always comes for Easter. What parts of the story are they missing, from Palm Sunday and the Three Days? Are those parts of the story important? What do those parts of the story tell us about God?

Easter

When is it? The date of Easter is the Sunday after the first full moon following the spring equinox (March 21). The dates for Lent and the Three Days are then fixed according to the date of Easter. The season of Easter lasts for seven weeks, or about 50 days. The Sunday after the final Sunday of Easter is Pentecost. The colors for Easter Sunday and the season of Easter are white and gold.

What is it about? Easter Sunday is the day we celebrate the Resurrection of Jesus Christ and his triumph over death and the grave. It is the most joyful day of the church year!

How do we celebrate it? On Easter Sunday, many people will wear white and bright colors, and maybe a whole new outfit. The church is decorated in flowers, especially Easter lilies, and other symbols of new life, like eggs and baby animals. There are special Easter hymns, and trumpets or a full brass section might make an appearance, to emphasize the celebration. Some churches may have a sunrise service that begins in a similar way to Holy Saturday but ends with the full story of the Resurrection.

What stories do we read from the Bible? On Easter Sunday, we read the story of the Resurrection. During the season of Easter, instead of having a reading from the Hebrew Scriptures each week, there is a reading from the book of Acts, instead, which outlines the history of the early Christian church. The Gospel readings during Easter are about what happened to Jesus and the disciples after the Resurrection.

1. Read Romans 8:31-39 in your Bible. (Verse 36 is a quotation from Psalm 44, reading Psalm 44:17-26 will give you context to understand it.) Try to rewrite this passage as

though you were explaining it to an 8 year old and be ready to share with the class.

This week I will pray for:

Faith Life

Priesthood of All Believers

Reading: Romans 12:4-14

Hymn: Rise Up O Saints of God ELW 669

Ministry of All

In the Middle Ages, there was an idea among many Christians that there were two classes of people: the sacred and the secular. The "sacred" were the priests and members of holy orders, whereas the "secular" were the everyday Christians. The sacred were perceived to be more holy, or closer to God, than the secular. This was an idea that Martin Luther especially wanted to dispel, holding that all the baptized were equal in the eyes of God.

The phrase "priesthood of all believers" came later on, and has come to summarize three ideas:

1. All Christians are equal before God, no one is more holy than anyone else.
2. No one needs to have another person as a "middleman" for their relationship with God.

3. While the church entrusts career ministry to those who are seen to have a call to it, all the baptized do some kind of ministry work, and we are all priests in that sense.

Luther was concerned about what he called the *good order* of the church: what might happen if a person who did not understand scripture tried to preach? Or what if a person who did not understand communion officiated a service with communion? He felt there should be some people who were especially well schooled in scripture and other relevant topics as clergy, and that there should be enough clergy so each Christian would have at least one easily accessible, for pastoral care as necessary.

However, he also understood that not all congregations might be able to have a pastor 100% of the time. If a pastor had a long-term illness, or if a church was extremely isolated, they would still need to hold services and have communion regularly. Based on this idea, there was a practice in the Lutheran church for hundreds of years that a congregation could "call" a member to be able to administer the sacraments, particularly communion, when the pastor was ill, traveling, or otherwise unavailable. The ELCA has recently altered that practice, with our agreement to be in full communion with the Episcopal Church in 1999, so that a layperson must have the express permission of their bishop to administer communion. We still believe this isn't necessary, but it was important to the Episcopalians, and sharing communion with our fellow Christians was the priority. (See 1 Corinthians 8 if you're curious why.)

1. Ever heard the phrase "holier than thou"? Can you think of a time when one person seemed holier or closer to God than another to you? Can you see how that idea could be dangerous?

Equal in Calling

This idea that all the baptized were equal before God was revolutionary in Luther's day. Remember, this was Germany in the 1500's: Europe was run by nobility and royalty, the hierarchy of the church had been a major international power for over a thousand years, and people had strict understandings of rank that were vital to how society worked. Who you could marry, where you could live, which professions you could enter - all were dramatically affected by who your parents were. Even within the church, your rank, wealth, and status affected how you were treated.

So Luther's claim that all Christians were made equal in baptism - farmers and bishops, fishermen and royalty - was greeted with a mix of astonishment and horror. This idea wasn't the only cause, but the reaction to it did contribute to the German Peasant's War of 1524-1525, the largest popular uprising Europe would see until the French Revolution. Untrained, uneducated peasants revolted against the conditions imposed on them by the aristocracy and were slaughtered by the thousands. Luther was horrified by the senseless violence, and especially those who took advantage of the situation for their own gain. This would not be the only time this concept would lead to violence: it would also contribute to American Revolution, begun on the idea that "all men are created equal."

Today, we tend to talk about this concept in terms of *vocation*. If a job is a paid position you have for a time, and a career is a lifetime of jobs of a certain type, a *vocation* is a job or career (or volunteer position, or life role) that you are called to; you feel you're supposed to do this work and find fulfillment in it. *Voca* in Latin, means "to call." This kind of call is very similar to the call to career ministry, in that there are both inner and outer calls. An inner call is based on a person's feeling directed to take up that role; some describe it as a "tug." An outer call is the recognition by others that this person has the skills, talents, and abilities to take on that role. A person might have one without the other - not everyone who feels called to enter the military is physically qualified to do so; and not everyone with the math skills to become an accountant feels called to it. Some people spend years looking for their *vocation* only to discover it isn't a career at all, but rather a role they play in some other part of their life.

1. Make two lists: the careers, and life roles aside from work, you'd find easy to believe as vocations, and those you doubt would be a vocation. What are some differences between them?

Counter-Cultural Ministry

In many times and places over the years, various people have tried to insist that Christianity was only something you did on Sundays: if you went to church, you were Christian, and if you didn't, you weren't. But the idea that Christianity is something that can be contained by a building, or that it doesn't apply to life outside of worship services, denies the life-changing power of the Gospel. The good news of God's grace and promises to us affect every aspect of our lives, every day of the week. Because of this, Christians engage in everyday ministry, separate from spiritual disciplines like Bible study or fasting.

The everyday ministry we engage in looks different for everyone, but it is often *counter-cultural*. That is, it goes against the popular culture. For example, in America, the popular culture tells us to value people according to social status markers: financial status or physical traits, among others. As Christians who believe that all people are beloved creations of God, when we refuse to treat people differently because of these markers, we are acting *counter-culturally* and performing Christian ministry. Or in a culture that tells us to lie when necessary in order to get ahead, or to place one's own needs ahead of anyone else's, truthfulness and generosity are *counter-cultural* acts of ministry.

This kind of ministry can take many forms. It might be telling the truth when it would be more convenient to lie; or standing up for someone being bullied. It could be refusing to treat people differently because of what they own or don't own; or calling someone on it when they make a racist joke. The old proverb, "What is right is not always popular, and what is popular is not always right" is a little overused, these days, but it remains true. Christianity isn't always an easy journey to follow.

1. When was the last time you had an opportunity to practice counter-cultural ministry? Did you?

This week I will pray for:

Spiritual Disciplines

Reading: Acts 2:42-47

Hymn: Lord Whose Love in Humble Service ELW 712

Acts of Commission

An *act of commission* is something you do on purpose- for example, choosing to come to Confirmation is an *act of commission*. Spiritual disciplines that are *acts of commission* include worship, prayer, serving others, and studying the Bible. Stewardship as well, we'll have a separate session on that.

Perhaps the two best known spiritual disciplines are worship and prayer. Certainly, both can and should be practiced individually, but Christians also put an emphasis on practicing them in community, because Christianity is by its nature a community-based faith. Who we choose to worship with, who we choose to pray with and for, says a lot about how we understand the Christian faith, and who we consider to be Christians and children of God. Worship and prayer as community allows Christians to support one another, to learn about community concerns and how to help, and to hear new ideas.

Service to those in need was the original Christian spiritual discipline. When Christianity began, it was one of few religious traditions outside of Israel that praised *altruism*, or unselfish care for the needs of others. (Judaism did as well, but there were fewer Jewish people outside of Israel then.) In that time without modern medicine, injury, disease, and poverty were an almost universal part of life. Helping those in need, without asking them to prove that they had "earned" that help, was shocking to many. Christians nursed the sick in epidemics, fed the poor without asking for anything in return, and cared for those who had no one to help them - and this was part of why Christianity began to spread like wildfire.

Bible study is often a spiritual discipline that people will feel they "should" do more of but are at a loss when it comes to how to go about it. One of the secrets of Bible study is to not expect to learn all the answers right away! Questions are a normal, expected part of Bible study. If you're looking for a place to start, I would suggest picking a Gospel and working your way through it in small pieces. If you're looking for a "method" or a way to organize your thoughts while doing Bible study, try these symbols:

→ - an idea to apply to daily life ! - this is important

↑ - what we are saying to God   O - overall concept of passage

↓ - what God is saying to us   ? - I have a question about this

1. Think back and write down the last time you practiced each of these spiritual disciplines. Where were you? Who were you with? Which would be easier to try with a group? Alone?

Acts of Omission

An *act of omission* is something you intentionally *don't* do - for example, choosing to *not* take the last slice of pizza is an *act of omission*. There are several spiritual disciplines that include *acts of omission*, such as fasting, keeping the sabbath, or practicing solitude or silence as a spiritual discipline.

The two forms of fasting you may be most familiar with are the concept of "giving something up for Lent," or a short-term fast to raise money for world hunger charities- the 30 Hour Famine or similar causes. Fasting doesn't have to be connected with food. A person could choose to fast from TV for a weekend, and spend that time reading the Bible as a spiritual discipline. Fasting is sometimes practiced in ways other than a spiritual discipline, including dieting and simplifying one's life. Fasting as a spiritual discipline involves abstaining specifically in order to focus on faith and draw closer to God.

Keeping the sabbath is a spiritual discipline that's become less obvious in the last 200 years. For centuries, it was common practice for Christians around the world to do as little work as possible on Sundays - animals had to be cared for and people had to be fed, but all work that wasn't strictly necessary was avoided until Sunday was over, including schoolwork! This is sometimes a plot point in stories set during that time period (for example, *Johnny Tremain* or *Anne of Green Gables*). Other activities were often not allowed as well- reading books that weren't faith-related, loud or rambunctious physical games, or shopping. Sundays were for church, Bible study, and rest, or restful activities only. Recently the positive effects of a day focused entirely on rest and faith have been recognized again.

Solitude & silence are sometimes misunderstood spiritual disciplines, which are somewhat related to fasting. Practicing these does not mean being a hermit. Many people practice these occasionally, and when they are used to encourage your faith, they are a spiritual discipline. Perhaps you have a short time each day when you turn off all electronics and sit in silence for a few minutes to listen for the voice of God, as a part of prayer time. Taking a day or a weekend to be alone, away from the noise of everyday life, could help you focus on a question or problem related to your faith.

1. What distractions could you fast from periodically to focus on your faith? (Other than food!)

Sharing the Gospel

Evangelism is a specifically Christian term, and it means "sharing the Gospel" (*evangel* is the Greek word for Gospel). Sharing this good news of God's love for us, is something we've been instructed to do by Jesus in the Bible. The most famous Bible passage about it is called the Great Commission: Jesus said, "Go therefore and make disciples of all nations, baptizing them in the name of the Father and of the Son and of the Holy Spirit, and teaching them to obey everything that I have commanded you. And remember, I am with you always, to the end of the age." (Matthew 28:19-20)

To do evangelism well, a strong code of ethics is required. Christian faith cannot be forced onto anyone and evangelism must be carried out with a relationship based on respect and trust. It's taken the church a long time to learn this lesson, and there are many stories from history of those who tried to spread the Christian faith through violence or imperialism. The Spanish Inquisition, the Native American boarding schools in North America, and many charities that have refused help to those who don't claim the Christian faith, are all examples of attempts to force faith on others. We've come to understand this lack of respect hurts not only those being forced into the church, but those already in the church, too.

In 2011, 3 Christian groups which together account for about 90% of Christians released a document: "Christian Witness in a Multi-Religious World: Recommendations for Conduct." It calls all evangelists to act with honesty, humility, and compassion, and without arrogance, condescension or insult. Violence, discrimination, and psychological or social pressure are rejected. Finally, in order to build relationships of respect and trust, inter-religious relationships without any hidden agendas are encouraged, to help cooperation and understanding. This document is online and about 5 pages long.

1. That last time you really disagreed with someone, but still understood their point of view: did you still try to persuade them? How did you (or could you have), while still respecting them?

This week I will pray for:

Stewardship

Reading: Deuteronomy 26:1-11

Hymn: Take My Life That I May Be ELW 685

What's Stewardship?

Stewardship is the name of another faith practice. A *steward*, in Biblical times, was a servant of the landowner, who managed all the owner's resources- crops, livestock, people, and money. The landowner had to trust this person, who was responsible for record-keeping and finances. Similar positions still exist in many companies today. This person would be a high-ranking employee- often a second-in-command who manages practical concerns and logistics. To be a steward is to be entrusted with a lot of power - a bad steward could embezzle or bankrupt their employer through incompetence.

Stewardship - or resource management - has always been an emphasis in churches, because managing the resources available is what allows for the work of ministry to continue. It has also come to include the concepts of fundraising, and "time and talent" management, especially in American churches. The state churches of Europe have been funded through taxes for centuries, but since America has no state-established religion, churches have had to fundraise in order to support their ministries.

Stewardship methods, and what stewardship focuses on, are often affected by events outside of the church. For example, before World War 1 many churches gave heavily to international missions and benevolence funds, with church building upkeep coming in a distant second. After the tragedy of the first World War, there was a sharp downturn in America's idealism and hope for international cooperation. Interest in international missions faded, and there was a boom of church buildings built in America as congregations focused inward, intent on maintaining their status through buildings and endowments.

Today, as church membership is no longer a standard social expectation in America, churches are filled not with people who feel they have to be there through social pressure, but instead with people who want to be there due to their faith. The related change in stewardship has been slow but steady- churches are focusing less and less on maintaining "how it's always been" and instead focusing on "how can we share the Gospel and help our neighbors?"

1. Consider your talents, time, and treasure. How do you steward them? Are you a good steward?

First Fruits

The idea of *first fruits* being given to God originated in ancient Israel, long before Jesus' time. The Israelites, after being brought out from slavery in Egypt by God, resettled Israel, called the "land flowing with milk and honey" because the farmland was so rich. In thanksgiving for being saved from slavery, and in acknowledgement of the abundance of the land they'd been given, Israelites brought the *first fruits* of each harvest, the best of the early part of their harvest, to the Temple.

The reason for focusing on first fruits in particular, was simple. Offerings at the Temple were the standard way to give thanks to God for what you'd been given. After all, even the best farmer can't grow much without the rainfall and good soil, which they did not create themselves. All that we have, we have been given by God. Greed may have tempted the farmers to wait until the end of the harvest, gather all the worst-quality of their crops together, and give that to the Temple, in order to make more of a profit off selling the best of what they grew. But that wouldn't be much of a thank you to the God who made all those crops possible in the first place. Israelites who weren't farmers could practice their stewardship in a similar way, offering their best to the Temple. And today, many people still practice giving their *first fruits* to God by having their donations to church as the first item on their budget they pay.

Eventually, as we moved out of a barter-based agricultural economy, into one that was based more heavily on currency, the concept of the *tithe* solidified. The idea of a tithe is that you give a set percentage of your income to a good cause. It is used most often to talk about money given to churches, and the traditional percentage associated with it is 10% as the words *tithe* and *tenth* are related, but it doesn't have to be either of those. Being able to tithe a set percentage of income requires budgeting and planning ahead, and this encourages people to give steady support to church instead of occasional gifts as they happen to be able to afford. This helps the church to plan ahead for what they will be able to afford.

1. Why might giving a set *percentage* of your income might be better budgeting than a set *amount?*

Gifts & Creation

Even today, in our society that is so obsessed with money, we recognize that there are other types of stewardship than the strictly financial. Separately from stewarding our money, we also must steward our time and our talents in order to provide the best possible resources for sharing the good news of the Gospel with the world. Giving of one's time might look like several different things-not only being present and participating in worship services, but also performing the many necessary tasks to keeping a congregation going. Some of these tasks are not glamorous, or indeed, very noticeable to those who don't know to look for them. They might include daily locking and unlocking of doors, stuffing envelopes, setting up for worship, cleaning up after an event, or caring for the church grounds. There are many tasks, which don't require financial resources or years of practice at a skill, that the work of ministry requires.

When we talk about stewarding our talents, many people often think first of those who have certain types of talents. Those who are gifted in public speaking, music, or social networking are often the center of attention when they're using their gifts. But those are not the only talents we have to steward, and many people with a gift don't even recognize it as one until it's pointed out to them. Galatians 5:22-23 lists the fruits of the Holy Spirit as "love, joy, peace, patience, kindness, generosity, faithfulness, gentleness, and self-control." Each of these gifts is a talent that is necessary to the work of the church! Those who visit the sick or imprisoned must have lots of love to give. Those who work on committees need both patience and self-control to get things done. Those who welcome visitors need kindness and generosity. And all of God's people need faithfulness to support each other in the work of the church.

Finally, the Bible also spends a lot of time talking about the stewardship of Creation. (There's a study Bible focused on this: The Green Bible.) God gave Creation to us as stewards, in Genesis 1:28, "have dominion over the fish of the sea and over the birds of the air and over every living thing that moves upon the earth." The word the NRSV translates as *dominion*, can also be translated *stewardship*. In gratitude to God for the many gifts we've been given through the gift of Creation, from atoms to whole galaxies, it is our duty to take good care of this gift, so it may continue blessing generations to come.

1. Take a walk around the church and look for signs of those unnoticed jobs that need doing. Do you know who does them? Are they something you could do, right now?

This week I will pray for:

Worship Whys

Reading: Revelation 2-3

Hymn: Holy Holy Holy Lord God Almighty ELW 413

What's "Liturgy"?

The word liturgy (**lit**-*ur-jee*) means the structure of worship. A worship service, whether weekly, or a marriage or funeral, has a shape and order to it, and this is its liturgy. Liturgy can include both music and spoken words, readings from scripture, or any other ritual about the worship of God. *Liturgical* churches, including many ELCA congregations, stress the participation of the congregation in the service, by pre-written prayers and responses to scripture, and a consistent structure.

Some denominations or congregations describe themselves as *non-liturgical*. Many Quakers practice what they call *waiting worship*, which has a predetermined time and length of meeting, but nothing is planned in advance. Worshipers sit in silence, listening for God's word and waiting for someone to be inspired to share something with the group: a scripture reading, or a hymn, or a prayer of their own devising. Other *non-liturgical* congregations simply have less of the exact wording of the service pre-planned, in order to allow the Holy Spirit to intervene. Many will always say the Lord's Prayer together, but the rest of the prayers may not be pre-written. The general structure of the service may remain similar, but often involves less congregation participation than liturgical worship.

A person who grew up in a liturgical church and went to a Quaker *waiting worship* service, might find it a surprise, or a *non-liturgical* service with little participation might feel more like a concert than a worship service. Preferring one type of worship to another doesn't make a person a better or worse Christian, but it impacts the way you think about what worship is about.

1. The ELCA's hymnal is called Evangelical Lutheran Worship, or the ELW, and it came out in 2006. Each section begins with a piece of artwork, what scenes do you see illustrated?

Sunday Services

Much of the liturgy from the services in the ELW is taken from various Bible verses, and the rest comes from ideas based in scripture. Check out the Scriptural Index on ELW p. 1154. We begin with the **Confession and Forgiveness**, because we are reminded in 1 John 1:8-9 that, "If we say that we have no sin, we deceive ourselves, and the truth is not in us. If we confess our sins, God who is faithful and just will forgive us our sins and cleanse us from all unrighteousness." One absolution is from Ephesians 2:4-5: "But God, who is rich in mercy, out of the great love with which he loved us even when we were dead through our trespasses, made us alive together with Christ—by grace you have been saved...."

The **Greeting** is taken directly from 2 Corinthians 13:13, "The grace of the Lord Jesus Christ, the love of God, and the communion of the Holy Spirit be with all of you." The **Kyrie** ("Lord, have mercy...") is borrowed from several Gospel stories. The two **Praise Canticle** options, "Glory to God" and "This is the Feast" have more direct references: Luke 2:14, "Glory to God in the highest heaven, and on earth peace among those whom he favors!" and Revelation 5:12-13: "Worthy is the Lamb that was slaughtered to receive power and wealth and wisdom and might and honor and glory and blessing!"

We sing **hymns** because the Bible instructs us to, including Psalm 149:1, "Praise the Lord! Sing to the Lord a new song, his praise in the assembly of the faithful." We read the **Bible** as instructed in 1 Timothy 4:13, "...give attention to the public reading of scripture, to exhorting, to teaching." Our **Gospel Acclamation** is from John 6:68, "Simon Peter answered him, 'Lord, to whom can we go? You have the words of eternal life.'" After the **Prayers** (there are countless Bible verses about prayer) we share the **Peace**, using Jesus' words from John 20:19, "Jesus came and stood among them and said, 'Peace be with you.'" This is before the **Offering** because of Matthew 5:23-24, "So when you are offering your gift at the altar, if you remember that your brother or sister has something against you, leave your gift there before the altar and go; first be reconciled to your brother or sister, and then come and offer your gift."

The **Holy Holy Holy** is taken from two parts of scripture, Isaiah 6:3, "And one called to another and said: 'Holy, holy, holy is the Lord of hosts; the whole earth is full of his glory.'" and Matthew 21:9, "The crowds that went ahead of him and that followed were shouting, 'Hosanna to the Son of David! Blessed is the one who comes in the name of the Lord! Hosanna in the highest heaven!'" The **Words of Institution** are directly from 1 Corinthians 11:23-26, "...the Lord Jesus on the night when he was betrayed took a loaf of bread, and when he had given thanks, he broke it and said, 'This is my body that is for you. Do this in remembrance of me.' In the same way he took the cup also, after supper, saying, 'This cup is the new covenant in my blood. Do this, as often as you drink it, in remembrance of me.' For as often as you eat this bread and drink the cup, you proclaim the Lord's death until he comes." The **Lord's Prayer** is from Matthew 6. And the **Lamb of God** is from John 1:29, "The next day he saw Jesus coming toward him and declared, 'Here is the Lamb of God who takes away the sin of the world!'" The service closes with the **Benediction**, one is taken directly from Numbers 6:23-26.

1. Look up Numbers 6:23-26 in your Lutheran Study Bible. What do the notes tell you about this?

Affirmation of Baptism/Confirmation

When you were baptized, your guardians and sponsors made many promises to you, and the assembly of Christians present would have promised to support you in your faith life. These promises are mirrored during the Affirmation of Baptism service, often called Confirmation, which happens during a weekly worship service, so that as much of the congregation as possible can be present to support the *confirmands* (people ready to be confirmed). Each confirmand is presented to the congregation, and a prayer of thanksgiving is given for them. Everyone present renounces the devil and all the forces that defy God, the powers of this world that rebel against God, and the ways of sin that draw us from God. Then the pastor will ask all present, including the confirmands, if they believe in God, and all respond with the Apostles' Creed. This is the confirmands *confirming* their Christianity.

But having faith is not all of what it means to be a Christian, so the confirmands make a series of promises, in response to the *covenant* (solemn promise with requirements) God made to them in their baptism. These promises include continuing to participate in Christian community, to attend worship services (including hearing the scriptures read and receiving Holy Communion), to share the gospel (good news) with others through words and actions, to serve all people with humility, and to work for justice and peace around the world. Then the congregation promises to support and pray for them. Finally, the pastor gives a blessing to each confirmand, and the congregation welcomes them into adult membership.

1. We don't do this renouncing very often, usually at Confirmations and Baptisms. How is this different from the Confession and Forgiveness that's often at the start of a worship service?

This week I will pray for:

Special Services

Reading: Ruth 1:6-18

Hymn: For All the Saints 422

Healing

Healing services are an ancient tradition of the church, and often taken place in two contexts: during a regular worship service, or in a personal visit by a pastor or a member of a social ministry team to a person who is in need of healing. The second type dates back to the Bible and is mentioned in James 5:14-15. Sometimes the healing that is looked for is of a physical nature, other times it's more mental or emotional. Occasionally the healing needed is a strong reminder of the power of God's forgiveness. These services take on many forms, but the format given in the ELW is meant for a worship service setting.

There are two special elements often included in a healing service: laying on of hands, and anointing. The laying on of hands is a Christian tradition that's often also used by communities sending a person or group out into service, or at weddings or ordinations, as a sign of the community's support of the people involved. In a healing service context, it reminds us of how people in the Bible were able to spread God's healing love through their touch. Recent studies have shown that those who experience supportive physical touch on a regular basis (hugs, handshakes, laying on of hands) tend to heal faster.

Anointing, usually by putting the sign of the cross in oil on a person's forehead, has a slightly different emphasis. In the Bible, we read of kings and prophets being anointed for their work and position. Anointing has a emphasis of *purpose* to it. Anointing can remind us that we are healed not just for the sake of being healed, but also to better share the love of God with all people.

It's important to emphasize that the healing service does *not* take the place of medical treatment. A healing service may lead to a miracle of physical healing, but one of the defining characteristics of a miracle is its unpredictability. Instead, a healing service is to remind us of the continued love and presence of God in our struggles, which is especially important in cultures where sickness or struggles are seen as signs of being forsaken by God. They also illustrate God's gifts of peace, strength and comfort as embodied by the Christian community. Miracles are certainly hoped for, but not counted on.

1. Think of someone you know who is in need of healing. What type of healing do they need: physical, emotional, mental, social, etc.? What would you pray for: strength, comfort, peace, etc.?

Weddings

A wedding is often very similar to a regular worship service, but there are four parts that only appear in weddings. These are the Declaration of Intent, Vows, Exchange of Rings, and the Marriage Blessing. The declaration of intent is when the couple declares that they intend to marry. This also implies that they're not already married to anyone else, though now that's taken care of with the marriage license.

Some couples write their own vows, others choose to use traditional vows. Two options are provided in the ELW. There are at least three promises essential to marriage vows: that the marriage is intended to last as long as they are both alive, that they will be faithful to each other, and that they will support one another in good times and bad. Sometimes vows will include other promises as well, including promises of respect, honesty, and trust. There is one promise that is never in marriage vows: the couple is *not* promising to be happy for the rest of their lives. No marriage is entirely without struggle. For many centuries, women getting married often had to promise to obey their husbands. Today, as a way to mark an understanding of marriage as an equal partnership, many couples exchange identical vows.

Many couples choose to exchange rings at their wedding. The rings serve as a sign to others that they are married, and a reminder to themselves of their relationship that they can carry with them. The pastor will say a prayer over the rings before they're exchanged. As the couple exchanges the rings they may use the words, "I give you this ring as a symbol of my vow. With all that I am, and all that I have, I honor you, in the name of the Father, and of the Son, and of the Holy Spirit." This acknowledges that their relationship is another way that they can show the love of God to others.

Finally, the marriage blessing is a further way to illustrate how a marriage can be an illustration to others of the love of God. God is thanked for the many blessings we've been given, and the Holy Spirit is asked to descend upon the couple with peace and love.

1. Think of one or two of your favorite hymns and praise songs. What topics are they about? What do they ask God for? Would they be appropriate things to sing about at a wedding?

Funerals

Many people tend to think of funerals as being of two types. When for an elderly person, who lived a full life before they died, the funeral may be seen as a celebration of their life. It can be a happy event: though those present will miss the person, this service is about how grateful we are to have known them. The second type of funeral that people think of, is the funeral that is for a tragic and unexpected death, perhaps for a young person who died of an illness or accident. This funeral helps the family and friends sort through their grief and anger about what has happened, to move past the first shock of the news and into healthy grieving. A "memorial service" means that the casket or urn is not actually present for the service. One might be held in another location, if the person lived far from their family.

A Christian funeral service often focuses on baptism, as we acknowledge all baptismal promises are fulfilled. So, Romans 6:3-5 is quoted in the ELW: "Do you not know that all of us who have been baptized into Christ Jesus were baptized into his death?... For if we have been united with him in a death like his, we will certainly be united with him in a resurrection like his." At a Christian funeral, there is sometimes both a *eulogy* and a sermon. The *eulogy* is a remembrance of the person: memories of events, their personality, and how they helped other people are shared. Sermons preach the good news of Jesus Christ's death and resurrection, and what that means for us. A funeral is often the time we need to hear that most. There are some funerals that especially focus on a sermon rather than a eulogy, if people had difficult relationships with the deceased. Focusing on God's love can be especially helpful then.

A Lutheran funeral service ends with the Commendation. To *commend* someone means to entrust them to another person, in this case to God, acknowledging that they are now entirely in God's care and not ours. The Committal, or graveside service, may happen just after the funeral or at another time. There are a few prayers and a final blessing. Lutherans & most Christians don't have a religious preference between burial or cremation, though the body returning to creation, whether through burial or scattering of ashes, is important to many ("earth to earth, ashes to ashes, dust to dust").

1. You may have questions you've always wanted to ask about funerals. There is another lesson on death & grief, but if you'd like, you'll be able to ask questions anonymously during class.

This week I will pray for:

Special Topics

Lutherans & The Bible

Reading: Acts 8:26-40

Hymn: Thy Strong Word ELW 511

How We Read The Bible

The scriptures speak often of "the Word of God," but they are not only speaking of themselves. The Bible is only one of the three ways that the Word of God comes to us. First, of course, is Jesus Christ, described as the Word of God incarnate in the first verses of the Gospel of John. Then, there is the Word active and alive today in the world through the Holy Spirit, shared through words, charity, and love by all Christians. This includes prayer, preaching, and the gifts of the Spirit. Finally, the Word of God in the Bible is the third way God shares the Word with us. Translations change, and we occasionally find older copies of the scriptures in Greek and Hebrew with little differences, but the sturdy foundation of the Bible has changed little over the centuries and given us a solid background to understand the Christian faith.

When we approach the Bible, we may do so in different ways, with different goals. At times we approach the Bible *devotionally*, seeking to understand how God's Word applies to us, or perhaps looking for guidance or meditation. At other times we may approach the Bible *academically*, seeking to understand the world and culture of Biblical times, or hoping to memorize passages, or better understand the structure of the Bible itself. Either approach has its uses, and both are appropriate ways to treat the Bible. (You may find people who use the word *critical* instead of *academic*- they're not critiquing the Bible! It's another meaning of the word *critical* which means thoughtful analysis.) You may find yourself leaning more heavily towards one or the other, depending on your personality or interests.

Another way to think of the Bible is as a library, consisting of 66 books, each perhaps including one or several *genres* of writing. A *genre* is a style of writing with specific uses and intentions. Some of the Bible includes poetry, for example, and we might understand poetry differently than we do a historical narrative, so we will read the Psalms differently than the Gospels. The Bible also includes parables, prophecies, legends, legal codes, letters, sermons, and many other genres. We will also approach these *genres* and stories with differing viewpoints, which will impact our understanding of the Bible. Someone with an irresponsible younger sibling is probably going to read the story of the Prodigal Son very differently than someone who *is* an irresponsible younger sibling! Or someone who's not fond of poetry won't seek their devotional time in the Psalms the way a poetry-lover will. All of this is normal, but we must understand our own points of view, to understand how they impact how we read the Bible.

1. Write down some words that describe you, and what you like (your age, family, location, history, story type and activity preferences, etc.). How might they impact how you read the Bible?

Law & Gospel

Luther held that there were two themes always present in scripture: Law and Gospel. We find the Law in the Bible when we find descriptions of our failings and our limitations, and the ways which we fall short of God's hopes for us. (The many sections of legal code in the Bible, rules and regulations, are one aspect of this Law: we need the legal code because it helps us to avoid hurting one another, which we would do without it.) The Law is given to us as instruction: we can't strive to better share God's love if we don't recognize the ways that we fail to do so. The Law can frighten or depress us at times, but it becomes far less frightening when we remember why it's shared with us.

The Gospel, God's promise of salvation given to us in the death and resurrection of Jesus Christ, is a constant reminder throughout the Bible of God's steadfast love for us. We find Gospel over and over again, not just in the four Gospels of Matthew, Mark, Luke, and John; but throughout the Bible because God's promises of life and salvation to us are spread throughout the Bible. It would be a mistake to think of the Hebrew Scriptures as only Law or the New Testament as only Gospel, because both have both Law and Gospel woven throughout. (Which we happen to see more clearly, of course, will depend on who we are and under what circumstances we're reading the passage at the time.)

This constant presence of both Law and Gospel is one part of what Luther called *theology of the cross*, by which he meant that Jesus's death on the cross is the central focus of the entire Bible. This moment of history is a classic example of both Law and Gospel. Law, because we, humanity, put Christ on the cross and killed him to begin with; and Gospel, because Jesus overcame death and the grave to save us. *Theology of the cross* acknowledges the presence of both Law and Gospel in both the Word of God and the world. The

Law then calls us to help those in need and speak for the voiceless. Luther contrasted this with *theology of glory* (also called *prosperity gospel*), which ignores the presence of the Law and humanity's failings in order to focus entirely God's glory and love; with no place to acknowledge those we have failed or to help those in dire need.

1. Can you think of an example of a "scary text" in the Bible? What happens if you try to understand this passage as Law, meant to teach? Is there Gospel in this passage?

Plain Sense, Through Christ

Luther always encouraged Christians to look for the "plain sense" of the meaning of Bible passages. Some prophecies and parables are rather cryptic, and certainly changes in the world's culture have major impact on how we understand the ancient words of the Bible, but there is no need to go looking for "secret codes" or "extra messages" in the Bible. He was reacting against the medieval method of Bible study, which expected at least 4 meanings to each passage. Certainly, many Bible passages have more than one meaning to different people in different contexts (see previous mention of the parable of the Prodigal Son), but there's no need to go looking for a set number of them. The Holy Spirit will make various themes in the Bible alive to us as necessary, no numerology or secret patterns necessary.

Lutherans also understand that scripture interprets scripture. If we find a verse or passage that we do not understand, we can seek further understanding by reading more of the Bible. People and events are often mentioned and described at many points in the Bible, between both testaments, as are most themes. A *cross-referenced* Bible, which lists other references to an idea or person in the text, or a *concordance*, which is like a dictionary that lists themes, people, and events, and their mentions in the Bible, can be helpful for this. The better we understand what a passage means in its own time and context, the better we can understand what it means to us today.

Finally, as Christians, we read the entire Bible through the "lens" of Christ, in the light of Christ's death and resurrection. Whether we are reading the Hebrew Scriptures or the New Testament, our understanding of the Bible is always impacted by our status as Christians, part of the Gospel promise. This means that we may often understand parts of scripture differently than non-Christians. For example, both Jewish people and Muslims study parts of the New Testament, because they value Jesus as a teacher, but we read it differently than they do because of our faith in Jesus as the Son of God. There are also several useful articles in the glossy insert near the middle of your Lutheran Study Bible.

1. People have found many "secret messages" in the Bible over the centuries. Below are the first and last few verses of Psalm 46 (a Lutheran favorite, it may remind you of a hymn) as translated in the 1611 King James Version (KJV) of the Bible. Underline the 46th word from the beginning, and the 46th word from the end. Does this remind you of someone else who was living in England around this time?

God is our refuge and strength, a very present help in trouble.
Therefore will not we fear, though the earth be removed,
and though the mountains be carried into the midst of the sea;
    Though the waters thereof roar and be troubled,
though the mountains shake with the swelling thereof.
...
He maketh wars to cease unto the end of the earth;
he breaketh the bow, and cutteth the spear in sunder;

he burneth the chariot in the fire.
Be still, and know that I am God:
I will be exalted among the heathen, I will be exalted in the earth.
The Lord of hosts is with us; the God of Jacob is our refuge.

This week I will pray for:

The End of All Things

Reading: Revelation 20:11-21:8

Hymn: Wake Awake For Night is Flying ELW 436

Death & Grief

One of humanity's oldest questions is, "What happens when we die?" Even within Christianity, there are different ideas about the concepts of heaven, hell, final judgment, and what salvation actually looks like. (Discussion of the final judgment continues in the Revelation section below.) Often the most urgent questions come down to, "Where are my loved ones who have died, right now?" At the end of a funeral service, we commend those who have died into God's care, but many people want further answers. Are ghosts real (and what does Saul and the medium of Endor bringing Samuel back from the dead in 1 Samuel 28 say about that)? When Jesus promised the criminal in Luke 23 who he was being crucified with, that they would be together in Paradise that day, does that mean heaven and hell are places we go immediately after death? The Bible does not actually walk us through what happens to us immediately after death, and so we are left to trust in God's promises of grace and eternal life.

Many people get nervous about how to treat a person who is grieving, or what to say to a person who has just experienced the loss of a loved one. The best gift to a grieving person is usually to be there, to be physically present. Many people allow their nervousness about grief to lead to their avoiding being with a grieving person, and this isolation is very hurtful. Saying things like, "I'm so sorry, this is terrible," validates the other person's emotions and lets them know that you support them. Acknowledging that everyone grieves differently and allowing a person to grieve as they need to, rather than how others believe they should, is very helpful. For example, whether or not a person cries in front of others has nothing to do with the depth of their grief. Finally, offering continued support is vital. Acknowledge anniversaries and birthdays, and keep checking in.

There are some things that people say to the grieving, meaning the best, which can be very hurtful. Very often saying things like "___ is in a better place now" or "this will pass" can be heard as instructions that the grieving person should not feel sorrow, even if that's not how it was meant. Phrases like "God has a plan" or "God needed them in heaven" can make it sound like God intended to cause this person pain, which certainly isn't true. Finally, unless you have actually experienced the exact situation of loss that the other person has, never say "I know how you feel." Even then, that's best left for a private conversation when the two of you have some time together, not a passing comment.

1. How have you seen life after death portrayed in popular media? Books, movies, TV?

Heaven & Hell

Most of the Bible's references to heaven are about the bodily resurrection and God's creation of a new heaven and new earth after the final judgment, rather than what happens to us immediately after death. However, Jesus mentions heaven in a more immediate way once: in Luke 23:43 he promised the criminal who was being crucified with him "Truly I tell you, today you will be with me in Paradise." Consistently, heaven is described as being in God's presence, free from fear, pain, or sorrow.

Discovering what the Bible has to say about a Christian idea of hell can be even more difficult. The Jewish conceptions of the afterlife don't line up to popular culture's ideas of heaven and hell, and references to them in the Hebrew Scriptures can be misleading to those who haven't looked into the topic in depth. In addition, some New Testament letters written to a Greek audience, reference Greek ideas about the afterlife. Jesus speaks of hell only through metaphor, referencing Jerusalem's Gehenna valley. First condemned after being used by Moloch worshipers to sacrifice children, it was later used as a landfill, burned to reduce the volume of garbage. It was often called the "lake of fire" or "the pit."

Overall, the ideas that popular culture gives us about heaven and hell don't tend to agree with what is actually in the Bible. Some of the most popular ideas come from classical literature, such as the "circles of hell" from Dante's *Inferno*. Others come from a misreading of the Bible, as the idea of St. Peter at a set of pearly gates, waiting for the recently deceased, came from a description of the new Jerusalem after the Last Judgment with 12 gates, each made with a single pearl (Revelation 21:21).

1. In the original Greek of Luke 23:43, there is no comma; the Greeks didn't use commas much. The translators added the comma because Jesus uses the phrase "truly I tell you" often. How would the meaning of the sentence change if the comma was *after* the word "today"?

Revelation

The last book of the Bible often has its name misspelled: the title of the book is Revelation, and it's singular, not plural. This is a single *revelation*, or a revealing, not several of them. (The Greek word which *apocalypse* comes from, also means a revealing or unveiling.) The author of this book is named John, and traditionally he has been understood to be the author of the Gospel of John and the disciple of Jesus, but he never claims to be in this book. The book has been understood in several ways: as a coded history of Israel or telling of events in John's time, as a prophecy of the future, or as an allegory about the struggle between good and evil. The book begins with letters written to seven churches, about their strengths and weaknesses, and we can learn what a church should aspire to from those letters.

The following chapters contain visions, though as they follow the letters to the churches, many have assumed the intended audience is the same. John describes visions of God's final judgment of the world, including the judgment of all people by their works in life, and God's grace distributed through what John calls the *book of life*. This is followed by a description of a new heaven and a new earth, including a new city of Jerusalem, as God makes all things new after triumphing over evil.

In the last 200 years, a new emphasis has been put on the book of Revelation by some Christian groups, focusing on an attempt to understand the timeline of the "end times" or "last days," as they are variously called. This emphasis was popularized by John Nelson Darby and Cyrus Scofield, who had both become pastors after careers in law, and their school of thought is called *dispensationalism*, often discussing the "Rapture." This came from a very specific way of reading the book of Revelation and combining it with other Biblical texts, such as 1 Thessalonians 4. In recent years, the fiction series *Left Behind,* and several predictions of the coming of the end of the world, have brought these ideas back into the limelight. The Bible does clearly, in several places, point to a bodily resurrection which we are reminded of in the third article of the Apostles' Creed. However, the concept of the Rapture as described by Darby and Scofield, and the many timelines they constructed go far beyond the "plain sense" reading of the Bible that Lutherans strive for. Until we fully understand, we cling to Jesus' words that we shall know neither the day nor the hour of the final judgment. (Matthew 24:36, 25:13)

1. If you wrote your congregation a letter about their strengths & weaknesses, what would you say?

This week I will pray for:

Spiritual Self Defense

Reading: Ezekiel 34:1-6

Hymn: The Church of Christ in Every Age ELW 729

Healthy Faith Communities

Part of becoming an adult member of a faith community is learning how to encourage the community, itself, to be healthy. Just as we can individually be healthy physically or mentally, communities can also have healthy and unhealthy characteristics. As a member of a community (faith-based or not) it is a part of our responsibility to build healthy relationships and community and discourage unhealthy tendencies. In order to do that, we need to have an understanding of what makes for a healthy community, and be able to identify signs of trouble, abuse, or unhealthy relationships.

For example, a healthy relationship includes having respect for one another without fear. This applies both in an individual relationship, between two people, or in a larger community. If you are ever part of a community where you fear the group, for any reason, that's obviously a danger signal. A healthy community welcomes questions and differences of opinion, respectfully shared. A community that refuses to allow questions, or any differences of opinion, is not a healthy one. For example, a chess club may expect that most members will have an interest in chess, but it would be unhealthy of them to insist that all members play precisely in the same way, or that they only ever play chess together. Very often, a community that instills fear, or refuses to allow for questions or differences, does so because the group will not stand up to examination. A healthy community can thrive with questions and differences.

These are things we must be especially careful of in faith communities. We have a natural impulse to want to trust our church, since this is where we worship God. This personal and emotional connection means we want to see these communities as safe places, literal sanctuaries. If a person experiences an unhealthy congregation, it is likely to affect their trust both in God and in the larger church. So when we are in faith communities, we have to be careful to show respect for others and to be trustworthy in all we do. Any break of that trust can be truly hurtful, because of where we are.

1. Name some places you have an expectation of trust, and some you don't have that expectation.

Identifying Abuse in a Faith Community

Unfortunately, faith communities are not immune from having abuse occur within them. Public schools have increased education in recognizing certain types of abuse in recent years, so many people can recognize and name various types of physical and sexual abuses. Less commonly discussed is psychological abuse, which often manifests as verbal aggression, or acts of dominance or jealousy. Verbal aggression, such as shouting, or using insults, is something most of us have resorted to at some point. However, when it becomes a regular pattern used to control others, it becomes a method of abuse. Displays of dominance may include destroying an object in front of another person as an implicit way of saying "it could have been you." When used to control another's actions, this also becomes abuse.

When discussing psychological abuse, the word jealousy has a specific meaning that isn't always included in the word's common use today. We may occasionally say, "I'm so jealous of ___," when they have a new electronic gadget or piece of clothing we want-that's envy we're feeling, not jealousy. Jealousy is when a person demands exclusive access to something or someone. When you tell your sibling that they can't touch your stuff, that's jealousy on a small scale. Like verbal aggression, jealousy of people becomes an act of abuse when it's used as a pattern to control behavior. We may be most familiar with this in the context of a romantic relationship, but it can also happen in other settings.

A few of the most obvious types of abuse which may appear in faith communities include shunning, isolationism, secret knowledge, and financial exploitation. *Shunning* punishes a member of the community by cutting them off from the community. Members are not allowed to speak or interact with this person, including their family. *Isolationism* is when a community forces their members to cut ties with the world outside their community, including family and friends who aren't members, which also makes it more difficult for members to leave the group. *Secret knowledge* or agendas, kept only to a select few, can keep regular group members in the dark about what the group is really up to. Finally, *financial exploitation,* either demanding members donate most or all of their resources to the group or forcing the members to work to support their group, keeps the members dependent on the group and discourages them from leaving. Abuse from trusted leaders of faith communities is often especially damaging and may cause a person to struggle with faith and the church for years to come.

234 | REV. KATHERINE ROHLOFF

1. Sports teams may use shouting and displays of dominance before a game, that they're going to win and they're better than the other team. Is this abuse? Why or why not?

What Makes A Cult?

The world "cult" should not be used lightly, but we cannot claim they don't exist. In his book *When Religion Becomes Evil*, Charles Kimball lists five characteristics of a cult: absolute truth claims; an insistence on blind obedience to authority and that the end result sought justifies any means used to get there; a focus on an ideal time and the declaration of a holy war. An absolute truth claim is not simply saying that what you say is the truth, which many religious groups (or other kinds of groups) do. An absolute truth claim says that not only is your claim the truth, but it is the only truth, the only possible correct understanding, to the exclusion of all others. An absolute truth claim includes the assumption that anyone who is not a part of your group is wrong by default.

An insistence on blind obedience to the group's authority, and the leaders of the group, goes back to the comments above about healthy communities thriving because of differences and questions. When the rules change from "do this, don't do this," to "do anything our leader says," that is a dangerous signal. Very often, in cult-like groups, this is paired with the idea that the end, or goal, that the group is working for, justifies any means, or method, used to achieve it. This is how many groups, religious or not, justify using violence or criminal acts to achieve their goals.

The concept of an ideal time is about a time in the future when everything will be perfect. For example, the new heaven and the new earth, created by God after the Last Judgment in the book of Revelation, is an ideal time. This concept in itself is not bad (or unusual), but it is the focus to the exclusion of everything else, it can become dangerous. When a group becomes so focused on this perfect, future time that they are willing to use violence or criminal acts to achieve it, or they are willing to ignore daily life in the present, that is a sign of extremism. This may also lead to the declaration of a holy war, which is either seen as literal war with violent conflict, or a war of ideas and arguments.

1. Do you think violence could ever make you agree with someone else on a religious matter?

This week I will pray for:

Oppression in the Bible

Reading: Matthew 15:21-28

Hymn: God of Tempest, God of Whirlwind ELW 400

Poverty in the Bible

They say that "money can't buy happiness" but it can buy a lot: food, shelter, education, and even the leisure time and communication resources it takes to become politically active in your community. Jesus speaks of feeding the hungry and visiting the sick and imprisoned, and says, "Just as you did it to one of the least of these who are members of my family, you did it to me," in Matthew 25:40. When we help those who are in need, we are acting out our Christian faith.

The Bible talks about how to help the poor in several places. For example, in Leviticus 19:9-10, the Israelites are told by God that when they harvest their crops, they must leave what's near the edges of the fields for those in need to come and harvest for themselves. (You may remember Ruth doing just that.) In modern times, now that many people don't live near farms, we often give to food banks as a way of living this out. In Deuteronomy 15:7-11, the people are instructed that when they give, they should do so generously and not grudgingly or with a "hard heart" so that the person helped won't cry out to God about it. This passage also mentions the Year of Jubilee, during which all debts were cancelled. This was important because back then, if you couldn't pay your debts, you became an indentured servant. The Year of Jubilee would end that time of service, and make sure no one was trapped in a cycle of endless debt. We're not sure how often this happened in ancient Israel, but it was supposed to be every 7 years.

In Mark 10:17-31, Jesus has a conversation with a rich man about what he must do to be saved. After the man claims to follow all the commandments, Jesus tells him to sell all he owns and give the money to the poor, which the man didn't want to hear. The disciples were confused, and ask, "Then who can be saved?" Jesus responds, "For mortals it is impossible, but not for God; for God all things are possible." Helping those in need is not something we do in order to **earn** God's grace and love- we already have those. Instead, helping those in need is a way to **share** God's grace and love with others. This shows up again in James 1:22-27, where the author of the letter encourages his readers to not only hear the word of God, but to act it out in their everyday lives. He says, "Religion that is pure and undefiled before God, the Father, is this: to care for orphans and widows in their distress, and to keep oneself unstained by the world." If we are "stained by the world" we might become jaded and hard-hearted about helping others, but if we give as God gives, we will do so generously and with grace.

1. Does it make a difference in how we help people, if we know or respect them? Is this Biblical?

Women in the Bible

The rights and status of women in ancient Israel change through the Bible: when Israel is strong, for example in Judges 4, women are allowed to become judges and we hear the story of Deborah. However, when Israel is weak and in danger, such as when they were led by Moses in the desert for 40 years, they had far fewer rights. One example is the 5 daughters of Zelophehad (*zel-off-eh-had*). They appear first in Numbers 27: their father Zelophehad has died, they have no brothers, and as women they had not been allowed to inherit anything. They tell Moses and Moses speaks to God, who says daughters with no brothers should inherit from that time on. But Moses doesn't give them their inheritance: instead they reappear in chapter 36, asking again. This time Moses speaks to several fellow leaders, who say that the women shouldn't inherit in case they marry men from different tribes, as then the wealth of Zelophehad's tribe would be given to others when they marry. Moses insists they marry only within their own tribe, and they do, but still he doesn't give them their inheritance. After Moses dies, the 5 daughters go to Joshua who has taken over after Moses' death, and he gives them their inheritance in Joshua 17.

The rights of women in Jesus' time were not much better. And yet, Jesus treated women with respect. Women, Mary Magdalene and others, were the first people to preach the Gospel, by sharing the good news that Christ was risen in Matthew 28, Luke 24, and John 20. When speaking of his coworkers in the church in his letters in the New Testament, Paul lists both women and men he's giving thanks for. In Romans 16:7, Paul greets Junia, saying she is "prominent among the apostles."

However, the church has not always treated Paul's coworkers with the same respect. An apostle was a person sent to preach the good news- similar to a pastor today. In some English translations of the Bible, Junia has been changed to Junias, a male name, on the assumption that a woman could not have had this role. Junia was a common Greek name for women from the time, and there are many documents outside of the Bible from that time and area that mention women named Junia. Yet there is no record of any men named Junias in that time and place. The church is still coming to realize the truth as Paul told us in Galatians 3, that we are all one in our baptism and, "There is no longer Jew or Greek, there is no longer slave or free, there is no longer male and female; for all of you are one in Christ Jesus."

1. "Feminism" means believing men & women should be treated equally by the law. How should they be treated by the church? Why?

Strangers & Foreigners in the Bible

As we read the Hebrew Scriptures, we see a contrast with our own society in how unexpected guests are treated. In Biblical times the law of hospitality - to provide for and protect any guests, whether invited or not - was very strong. The law of hospitality is implied every time the Bible talks about guests but is perhaps best shown in Genesis 18:1-8. Abraham is relaxing at home and suddenly three strangers arrive. Abraham immediately jumps up and hurries to provide them with a meal, without ever asking who they are or why they are there. In this desert culture, when water is scarce and travelers may be faced with many dangers, hospitality was always offered generously, because next time you may be the one in need. In the following chapter, Abraham's nephew Lot puts the safety of his guests ahead of the safety of his own daughters, taking the law of hospitality to an unusual extreme.

People of other countries appear frequently in the Bible, and not always happily. Deuteronomy 23 lists groups of people who are not permitted to attend worship, including Moabites. However, later we read the story of Ruth the Moabite in her own book of the Bible, and she becomes an ancestor of King David and Jesus. The

New Testament frequently mentions Samaritans, descended from the former northern tribes of Israel who have been cut off from the southern tribes near Jerusalem for generations. They are clearly not trusted by the Israelites and not counted as truly Jewish. Then Jesus tells the story of the Good Samaritan, and he and the disciples spend time in Samaria. It becomes clear, reading the Bible, that while all people are equal and welcome in God's eyes, we still see through our own eyes, and our prejudices still color our willingness to see one another as children of God.

1. If you went to church in another country, how would you hope to be welcomed?

This week I will pray for:

Science & Faith

Reading: Job 38:4-21

Hymn: Earth & All Stars ELW 731

Science & Faith: Complementary Perspectives

If you watch much TV, you'll notice that often science and faith are talked about as though they're in competition with one another. However, it is very possible to be a person of science and faith at the same time, and the two disciplines have much to offer the other. In fact, for generations theology (the study of God) was called the "Queen of the Sciences." Biology, chemistry, physics; they all study God's creation and God's gifts to us, and so the sciences themselves and the knowledge from them were seen as additional gifts from God. To study God was seen as a science: the most important one of all!

When we call them "complementary" perspectives, we're not talking about compliments, or that they are constantly saying nice things about each other. Instead, they complement each other, or complete one another by addressing different needs and ideas. One way of summing this up is to say that science addresses the question of **how**, and faith addresses the question of **why**. Science can tell us how the earth was formed, or how the dinosaurs died, or how a baby is made, but not why we are here. Faith can lead us to why we are called to love one another, but not how the sky looks blue to us.

So, science and faith both have much to offer to us, and to each other. It is through science we can better understand the "how" of God's creation, the extraordinary complexity of the cosmos we inhabit, and the wondrous variety of humanity. It is through faith we can explore what we are called to do with this knowledge, how best to use it for the good of all people, and what it will lead us to become. However, the very different ways that science and faith tend to approach related questions can lead to what seem like irreconcilable differences.

1. What parts of your life are governed by science? By faith? Shared by both?

God's Big Bang

The Big Bang is the current scientific understanding of how the universe began - that all the matter in the universe exploded outwards from a single point. This idea is called a *scientific theory*, which means that it has been well tested, using the scientific method, and has significant evidence supporting it. However, some Christians believe that, due to the creation accounts at the beginning of Genesis, this cannot be true. Generally, these Christians can be divided into two groups, Young Earth Creationists, and Old Earth Creationists.

Young Earth Creationists generally believe that the first creation account in Genesis is literally true: that the universe was created in 7 24 hour days by God, and that the timeline of events in the Bible is precisely accurate. This belief system does not allow for the Big Bang theory, evolution, or the existence of dinosaurs. An Irish Archbishop, James Ussher, calculated the genealogies and dates given in the Bible and determined that the moment of creation happened during the evening of October 24, 4004 BCE. When asked about the apparent age of the Earth or the existence of dinosaur bones, or related matters, Young Earth Creationists will often say that these things are tests of our faith from God.

Old Earth Creationism encompass a broad spectrum of beliefs - including those who embrace the Big Bang. Some state that the "days" given in the first chapter of Genesis were not literally 24 hours long and instead are metaphors for longer periods of time, but that the creation otherwise happened in the same order as given in the Bible. Others will say that what science tells us - the Big Bang, evolution and so forth - are true, but that these scientific understandings are God's way of creating the universe, and the stories in Genesis are allegories meant to tell that story to an ancient people without our scientific understanding. This is often referred to as "theistic evolution" or "evolutionary creationism."

The idea that the Genesis accounts of creation might not be literal, historical retellings dates back far longer than the Big Bang theory. In the third century, Origen, an early Christian scholar, wrote that the Genesis creation accounts must be allegories, since "day" and "evening" couldn't exist without a sky, sun, moon, and stars. The well-known Jewish rabbi, Moshe ben Maimon, or Rambam, said in the 1100s, "We do not reject the Eternity of the Universe because certain passages in Scripture affirm Creation, for it is neither impossible nor difficult to find for them a suitable interpretation. But the Eternity of the Universe has not been proved; a mere argument in favor of a certain theory is not sufficient reason for rejecting the literal meaning of a Biblical text." (Guide to the Perplexed 11,25) Therefore, Jewish people who feel the Big Bang **has** been proved are free to embrace it.

1. Take a look at the order of what is created when in Genesis 1. Does that match the order science tells us various things came to be? Does the order of the second account match the first?

Faith & Human Health

The ELCA has released 3 Social Statements related to human health: Caring for Health: Our Shared Endeavor in 2003; Human Sexuality in 2009; and Genetics in 2011. The health care statement concludes that health care cannot, for Christians, be primarily about profit, but must be about caring for those in need. This also means that we must take responsibility for our own health, however we can, in gratitude for our gift of life. The statement acknowledges that not all people receive the care they require under the current US health care system, but that true reform would be very complicated. The statement also discusses what healing means: it does not always mean coming into a state of perfect physical health, but can also include relationship with God and healthy community support. Being healed does not mean being free of pain and suffering; sometimes it's about relational or spiritual healing.

The Human Sexuality statement asks how we understand sexuality in the context of faith and our Christian identity. It affirms that sexuality itself is a powerful gift from God, and that as humans we need healthy relationships. In regard to scientific and health care issues, it acknowledges that education is key, and that the intensely personal nature of sexuality means that it can be difficult for us to discuss these questions as we would others. The statement encourages us to remember that we have all been created by God, and therefore any message insulting a particular body type or health condition, or that certain people deserve to be treated as property, does not come from God.

The Genetics statement acknowledges that the word "genetics" is not in the Bible, but that what we learn from the Bible can guide us in our decisions about genetic research and application. God calls us to be "imaginative stewards," and we are called to use our knowledge with compassion. Genetic research and application can help many people, but also includes dangers. We must act with respect for all people, with justice and wisdom, and not act out of selfish or profit-driven desires. We acknowledge our limitations and failings while also recognizing that we have been called by God to act with love.

1. When you're sick, do you pray? Do you go to the doctor? Do you do both? Why?

This week I will pray for:

Appendix: Bible Study Guides

The Holy Spirit being certain to show up in any Bible study, to lead you down paths you never expected, please take these questions (and especially the "*answers*") as a general guide rather than an exact map. You know your people, what questions they need to ask and what they need to hear, best. Most of these questions aren't the kind to have one perfect true answer, most of the answers included are just meant to point you in a direction if you get lost.

Five *Solas*: Lutheran Basics – Psalm 46

There are Bible passages mentioned next to each section title- if you have questions about the idea, these are good places to find more on where these ideas come from and what they're about.

Take a look at the Psalm. Does it sound familiar? This is the Biblical text Martin Luther used in his most famous hymn, "A Mighty Fortress." He didn't choose this Psalm at random- he spent his younger years terrified of God's anger, and after he broke away from the Roman Catholic Church, his life was often in danger. He needed a God who is a refuge from danger.

-verses 1-3 – What does "very present" mean? See the margin note on these verses in your AF Lutheran Study Bible. What kind of weather & natural disasters do v. 2-3 refer to? (*Earthquakes, sea storms.*)

-**v. 4-6** – Communities, in Biblical times and today, are often built near rivers. What city do you think is referred to here? (*Both Jerusalem, & New Jerusalem of Revelation.*)

-**v. 7, 11** – See the margin note at the top of p. 899

-**v. 8-10** – Do verses 8 & 9 contradict each other? (*Ending a war, especially as described in v. 9, might end in desolation- but is it a bad desolation compared to what was?*) If you rewrote the second half of v. 9 for today, what would it say? (*Replacing bow, spear, shield with modern weapons.*) Does this sound like a God who is a refuge?

Why Have Commandments? – Exodus 19:1-8

Read the 2nd paragraph of What's the Story at the beginning of the book of Exodus for background on what this passage is about.

-**v.1-2:** How long have the Israelites been traveling away from Egypt together? (*3 new moons, about 3 months.*) What was happening in your life 3 months ago, to get an idea of how long that is? What do we have when we travel now that they wouldn't have had? (*gas-powered vehicles, modern plumbing, internet & phones, travel toiletries, etc.*) They don't have a settled community, many belongings, careers, or many creature comforts- all things we use to define who we are. What do they have left to define who they are? (*language, faith, relationships*)

-**v. 2-6:** Read the margin note on "How do Lutherans see God's law?" Another way we define who we are, is by the rules with which we define our lives. Does your family have rules that other families don't, that help define who you are?

-**v. 7-8:** Who is speaking in verse 8? (*all the people*) Read the margin note "What is the priesthood of all believers?" Whose job is it to do ministry? (*all of us*)

Commandments About God – 1 John 4:7-16

-v. 7-9: Based on these verses, what's really important to God? (*love!*)

-v. 10-12: Did we have to do anything to earn Jesus coming to us? (*no, it was out of God's love for us*) Read the margin note on "Where does love of God and love of neighbor come from?" If we learn to love our neighbors from God's love for us, should our neighbors have to do anything to earn our love? (*no*)

-v. 13-16: Go back and look at v. 7 again- who "is born of God and knows God"? (*everyone who loves*) & v. 12- God lives in us if we love who? (*one another*) So when we say God lives in us, who is the "us"? (*everyone who loves one another*)

Commandments About Relationships – Mark 10:2-12

Before reading this passage, think about the people you know who have gone through a divorce. Do you trust them to make good decisions for themselves? Do they deserve to live in safety? What are some reasons a divorce might happen? (*abuse, adultery, growing apart, married for the wrong reasons*)

-v. 2-4: Go back & read Deuteronomy 24:1-4. Do these verses describe a relationship of equals? (*no, only one can divorce, & marrying another is described as being defiled*) See the margin note for these verses- women needed written proof they were divorced to marry again, men didn't. Since society didn't allow women to hold jobs to provide for themselves and their family, if a woman couldn't return to her own family for some reason, she needed to be able to marry again. Marriage was often more about economics than love, & women were often treated like property instead of people.

-v. 5-9: What is "hardness of heart" which Jesus mentions in v. 5? (*being uncaring, cruel*) Read v. 8 again- the relationship Jesus is describing, is that meant to be equal? (*if you become one then you have to be equal*) Read the margin note for verses 2-12- what was God's purpose for marriage? (*to become one, to share love learned from God with each other*)

-**v. 10-12:** There's historical context to these verses that can be easy to miss. Herod Antipas, who ruled this area on behalf of Rome at the time, had divorced his wife to marry Herodias, the wife of his half-brother, who had divorced her husband in order to marry him. John the Baptist spoke out against this and that lead to his execution. The Pharisees who asked Jesus about divorce, were probably less interested in his thoughts on marriage & more interested in whether he would say the same things John had said. But Jesus waited until they weren't around to say this. Is there a difference between divorcing one person in order to marry another, versus happening to marry someone who has previously been married? Does that difference involve being hard-hearted towards others?

Commandments About Community – Luke 18:18-27

-**v. 18-20:** In their first exchange, the "young ruler" seems to treat Jesus as just another teacher, & Jesus gives a standard, acceptable answer.

-**v. 21-23:** Now the young ruler makes an extraordinary claim- even if you're just taking the simplest understanding of these commandments rather than Luther's expanded understanding- can you say you've always completely honored your parents? So Jesus makes a demand of similar strength, and if the young ruler really is as invested in supporting his community as he's said he is by obeying those commandments, should it be hard for him to follow?

-**v. 24-27:** This is one of the few passages when Jesus speaks directly to and about the rich. We mostly see Jesus with the poor, those needing healing, the powerless. When he's around the poor

& sick & powerless, what's Jesus usually like? (*gentle, generous, grace-filled*) Does Jesus deal with the rich differently, and if so, why would he?

Creator Almighty – Genesis 1-2

The books of the Bible are divided up into chapters and verses- these mostly remain the same from one translation to the next. Another way the Bible is often divided is by section headings- these aren't from the original texts, so they might be in different places or say very different things in different Bibles.

-**v. 1:1**- What's the first section heading, in light blue, in this Bible?

-**v. 2:4**- What's the second section heading? So how many stories of Creation do we have here? See margin note for v. 2:4b-25.

-**v. 1:27 & 2:18**- For example, see these two verses, each of which introduce the creation of women. How are they different? (*in chapter 1, the woman is also created in the image of God and is never implied to be inferior, in chapter 2, the woman is created second and called a helper*)

-One common way to talk about the difference between the Bible and science textbooks, or faith and science, is that the Bible and faith are concerned with the question, "why?." while science asks the question, "how?" So the Bible doesn't always have a single, logically-proven answer to a question, and will sometimes include two versions of the same story, in order to give a more complete picture.

Jesus Christ – Philippians 2:5-11

Start with the margin note at the top of page 1932. Don't forget that these verses have been translated from Ancient Greek into English, so while they might not sound much like song lyrics or poetry to us, they would in the original language.

-**v. 5-8:** Think about the differences between being human and being God. If you were as powerful as God, what would you want to do? Would you want to give up all that and become human, and eventually die? So when we understand what Jesus was willing to do for us, what does verse 5 mean- what should our mindset be? (*humility, generosity, greatness of heart*) Does everyone who has faith in Christ, always have that mindset?

-**v. 9-11:** The phrases "every knee should bend" and "every tongue should confess" may sound familiar from hymns or liturgy. What would the world be like if everyone shared the mindset that Jesus had? What would be different?

Holy Spirit – Matthew 3:11-17

-**v. 11-12:** The speaker here is John the Baptist. Is fire always a scary image? See the margin note for v. 7-12. If wheat isn't commonly grown in your area, try retelling v. 12 as about corncobs and husks rather than wheat and chaff. Just as the corncob and husk (or wheat and chaff) start as one, but are separated, so we each begin as people with deep flaws & sin, which God will separate us from & destroy. This is not a verse about God destroying people, but about God purifying people. Fire is often a symbol connected with the Holy Spirit, such as in the Pentecost story in Acts 2.

-**v. 13-15:** "Righteousness" in the Bible often refers to properly fulfilling your relationship roles- being a good parent, child, friend, employer, etc. Jesus is both announcing that he's one of us by being baptized, just like we are, and that baptism is a true source of relationship with God, for us. See the note on v. 15 for more on righteousness.

-**v. 16-17:** In Matthew, Jesus' baptism is our introduction to him, the first time we see him as an adult- so God is introducing him. When we are baptized, just as when Jesus was baptized, we understand that the Spirit of God descends on us and God claims us as

God's beloved child. Our baptism serves as our introduction to the church, where the Holy Spirit is always at work.

Teach Us To Pray – Matthew 6:1-8

Try the Lectio Divina process with the Matthew 6 passage! There are several helpful guides online.

-v. 1-4: A person's *piety* is how they fulfill their religious obligations, which might include praying, reading the Bible, attending worship, giving to the poor, working for justice, and so on. A person who is *pious* is very careful and strict about doing that. According to v. 1, which should be more important to Christians- that they do these things, or that they are seen by others when doing these things?

-*Alms* are donations to those in need. What are some examples of alms we might give today? (*donations to food pantries, money to charities, our time & work to Habitat for Humanity, etc.*) According to these verses, should we care whether other people know about the alms we give?

-v. 5-8: So having read the earlier verses, is this part of the passage telling us that we should never pray in public? Can you pray in public without doing it for praise/admiration from other people? How can you tell the difference between someone who's following these verses, and someone who isn't when they say grace over their meal in a restaurant, or lead a group of people in prayer at a worship service, for example?

Addressing God – Deuteronomy 6:4-9

-v. 4-5: Most Christians are probably familiar with the Lord's Prayer, and John 3:16. These verses are the most well-known verses and prayer for the Jewish people, about as well-known as both of those are among Christians. See the margin note for v. 4-5. When Jesus is asked what the greatest commandment is, he quotes this verse, and then gives the Golden Rule, in Matthew 22:35-40 and Mark 28-34.

-**v. 6-9:** These verses list some ways that the people of God can show that these verses are important to them, and that they consider these verses in everything they do. If you were going to show the world that a certain verse or quote was important to you, how would you show it? (*social media, t-shirts, skywriting?*)

Our Needs – Psalm 23

Before you start, read the last 2 paragraphs of the "Background File" for the Psalms on p. 847. Then take a look at the many kinds of psalms listed on p. 849-850.

-**v. 1-3:** When we first met David in the Hebrew Scriptures, as the youngest of many brothers, what job did he have? (*shepherd*) See the margin note for verse 1. Ideally, what would the job descriptions of a shepherd and a king have in common? (*leading, protecting, caring for, providing for, etc.*)

-**v. 4-6:** When a shepherd carries a rod or staff, it's used to protect the sheep from predators, not to hurt them. What would it mean to you if someone powerful gave a banquet in your honor, and invited your enemies to it? What would your relationship with that powerful person be like afterwards?

-So reading this psalm, what words would you use to describe our relationship with God? What does God do for us?

Communion: What God Does – Luke 22:14-27

-**v. 14-16** – When, in the story of Jesus' life, is this Bible passage happening? Or maybe an easier question, do you recognize what church holiday this story is about? (*Maundy Thursday, Last Supper, day before Jesus died, etc.*) What does Jesus mean when he says, "Before I suffer"? (*His torture and death, but the disciples don't really realize* *that yet.*) See note A on v. 16 at the bottom of the page, also the margin note on Luke 4:43 about where God's will is done.

-v. 17-18 – When is the kingdom of God coming? (*When Jesus is resurrected – the kingdom is not something we are waiting for but something that is here which we encourage with our actions. If students ask about the sponge soaked in old wine held to Jesus' lips during his crucifixion, that is soured wine, which is wine that has turned to vinegar and is no longer wine.*)

-v. 19-20 – When during the meal do these verses happen? (*Jesus passes around the bread right after the table blessing at the beginning, and the wine after the meal is over.*) See the margin note on these verses.

-v. 21-23 – In this Gospel, Satan has entered into Judas by this point, which probably took away his ability to make decisions. (*See Luke 22:3.*) Why is Judas at the table with the other disciples here? Why wouldn't Jesus have kicked him out? Did Judas receive communion? What does that mean? (*We really don't know the answer to any of these, but the ideas people bring up will tell you a lot about what they think about grace and friendship. Playing a little devil's advocate with their answers to get them to say why they think what they think, can tell you even more, but don't push too hard. Questions about friendship and betrayal are often very emotional and you want to stay on topic. This will lead into the conversation in the next set of verses....*)

-v. 24-27 – That sounds like a quick topic change! Does it come out of nowhere or do you think it came out of what's been going on naturally? (*Conversation may center around Jesus' humility in giving his life for us, or Judas' pride in betraying Jesus.*)

– What does leading like a servant, as Jesus describes at the end here, actually look like in real life? (*If they have trouble with this, ask* what the opposite, leading with too much pride/snootiness looks like, and then think about the opposite.)

Communion: What We Do – Luke 8:42b-48

Before starting this section, it may be useful to point out the word "hemorrhage" and make sure the students know how to pronounce it and what it means. (*A flow of blood, you don't have to be more specific. Feel free to point out the difficulty of doing laundry in ancient Palestine compared to now.*)

-v. 42b-43 – (*Starting with "As he went...."*) The woman with the hemorrhages described in this passage would have been ritually unclean in addition to her physical problems, in that time and culture. This means she wouldn't have been able to worship in the Temple in Jerusalem, and there would have been lots of rules about who she could live and eat with, when. This wasn't the culture trying to be cruel to her- they didn't have our modern knowledge of how sickness works, so people who had certain physical difficulties that we'd think of as "possibly contagious" were isolated in certain ways. This woman would have been kept separate from much of her community and even family, a lot of the time, for this reason. Her being in a public crowd is an act of desperation and even rebellion, since if she touched someone, her ritual uncleanliness would spread to them. While they could cleanse themselves over the course of a few days, she would remain unclean as long as she had the hemorrhages.

-v. 44-45 – Now the woman has been healed, but she hasn't spoken to Jesus yet. Has she done anything to "earn" this? Has she somehow proven herself "worthy"? (*All she's done is touch Jesus' cloak, and that without permission- which according to the rules would have spread her uncleanness to him. She hasn't made an offering or statement of faith, at least with words, yet. We don't even know if she was sure this would work.*)

– Is Peter being reasonable here? (*Sure, but he doesn't really realize what Jesus is talking about yet- the flow of power.*)

-**v. 46-48** – Why was the woman trembling when she came to Jesus? Why would she try to remain hidden at first? (*She's scared, she's never met Jesus before, she doesn't know how he'll react to her asking forgiveness instead of permission yet.*) Why does she fall at his feet instead of standing and talking to him directly? (*She's begging, she's desperate, and she's asking forgiveness.*)

– Her "faith has made her well" – how? (*Jesus doesn't demand that we perform certain rituals or pray certain prayers to receive God's grace, which is a type of healing, we are saved by God's grace just through our faith.*)

Baptism: What God Does – Romans 6:1-11

-**v. 1-2** – What do these two verses mean, what is Paul suggesting and then refusing? Can you phrase it so an 8 year old would understand it? (*Since God's grace is good, should we sin more, so there's more grace? No! We've been saved from sin, why would we keep living in it on purpose?*)

-**v. 3-5** – These verses remind us of a church holiday, don't they? (*Good Friday & Easter.*) Why do you think we talk about baptism at funerals? (*We do die, like Christ died, but we will rise again on the last day, as Christ was resurrected. A funeral is the end of a person's baptismal journey, there's nothing left for them to "do," the next steps are automatic.*)

-**v. 6-11** – So we're dead to, or freed from, sin, does that mean we don't sin anymore? Does that mean we can do whatever we want? (*Yes, of course we sin, we aren't perfect, we are just saved from [some of] the consequences. [What we do will impact what other people do, so some consequences still stick.] No, why would we want to, see v.1-2 again.*) See the margin note on these verses about how baptism affects our daily life, especially the first sentence.

Baptism: What We Do – Matthew 28:16-20

-**v. 16-17** – When does this story happen in Jesus' life? Why are there only 11 disciples here? (*This is after Jesus has been resurrected, there are 11 because Judas is gone.*)

– What did the disciples doubt, and why? (*This is the first time they've seen him since his death, they aren't sure it's really him or that they believe the witness of the women.*)

-**v. 18-20** – What is a disciple, what does the word mean? (*Student of a teacher, in the Bible, Jesus' students.*) What's the difference between a disciple of Jesus, and a Christian today? (*The disciples met & walked with Jesus but weren't empowered to proclaim the gospel to the world until this passage, whereas we can do that as soon as we're baptized [though it helps if we can communicate with words, too].*)

– Where are we to follow Jesus' instructions given in v. 19-20? Is anyone left out of this? (*In "the nations," everywhere not-Israel [in addition to Israel, that instruction given earlier]. No, we are to proclaim the gospel to absolutely everyone, no one is left out.*)

Early Church to the Great Schism – Matthew 16:13-20

-**v. 13** – (*Pronounce "says-a-ree-ah fil-lip-pie."*) The title "Son of Man" means a few different things in the Gospel of Matthew, but it always reminds us that Jesus was both fully divine, the Son of God, but also fully human, just like us. This title also ties into the Hebrew Scriptures.

-**v. 14-16** – The disciples list a few prophets, all of whom were unpopular in their times because they said things people didn't want to hear. Is this something Jesus shares in common with them? (*He's* *going to die for it, so yes.*) Also see footnote A about the parallel between Son of God and Son of Man.

-v. 17 – Jesus is saying that Peter has been given this information by God directly, this isn't Peter having worked it out for himself through his own flesh-and-blood. Remember faith comes to us through the Holy Spirit, it isn't something we earn or do on our own.

-v. 18 – This is where Peter finally gets his name, the name Peter means rock, he was born Simon but from now on people will call him Peter. The author of the Gospel of Matthew knew this was coming and called him Simon Peter before this verse, but when Jesus gave him this name it was brand new. The name Peter didn't exist until this happened. See related sidebar about Peter becoming the first pope. When Jesus says the "gates of Hades will not prevail against it," that is the church, he's saying that death won't overcome the church.

-v. 19-20 – This is also referenced in the previous page's sidebar. This is a good time for a brief discussion of the Office of the Keys, though it's also in the Small Catechism. One of the ongoing themes in Matthew is that Jesus didn't want people to know who he was until the very end of his time on Earth. People have lots of ideas about why, do you have a guess? (*Maybe he wanted to not be constantly surrounded by large crowds, maybe not being as famous meant it took more time for the government to notice him so he had more time for ministry, maybe he wanted the full church to be built by the apostles and not himself?*)

Reformation – Ephesians 2:1-10

-v. 1-3 – See the margin note on v. 2 about who the "ruler of the power of the air" is.

-**v. 4-7** – Does this passage sound familiar? Most of the liturgy in our worship services come from various Bible passages, this is often used in the Forgiveness part of Confession & Forgiveness.

-**v. 8-9** – These are the verses that convinced Martin Luther, who grew up terrified that God must always be angry with him, that God truly loved him after all. So, reading these verses, can one person be "more holy" or "more saved" than another person? (*No, this is God's work, not ours. You may want to talk briefly about how sometimes it feels like some people are more holy than others anyway, and that those people are probably just as confused as everyone else, though maybe about different things.*)

-**v. 10** – People talk about doing good works as a part of faith a lot, even if they don't always use those words for it. Often, though, we hear that there are certain things that a person "must" do if they have faith, or must not do. But here it says that God created us "for" good works, not that our faith "requires" them. It's kind of like how many of us have hobbies or talents that we enjoy- but as soon as someone is making us do them, they aren't as enjoyable at all, are they? One of the ways Lutherans talk about this is to say that we are, "Freed from, and freed to." We are freed from sin, by God, so that we are freed to do good works, and do God's work in the world, and share God's love with others.

Lutherans & World War II – 1 Peter 2:11-17

Before you begin this Bible study, look over the Background File section for First Peter and select what information to share with the students as they open their Bibles.

-**v. 11-12** – How do these verses tell us to act when we are around non-Christians? (*Honorably, even if treated unfairly and rumors are spread about you.*) What does that look like in everyday life?

-v. 13-15 – When faced by the ignorance of the foolish, what are we supposed to do? (*Do right in the face of it, which will eventually silence the foolish as they become embarrassed of what they've done. Keep in mind the people the author was writing to, weren't powerful people, they couldn't make big changes on their own. The only way they could change things was by setting a good example.*)

-v. 16-17 – Here we see that saying, "only God can judge me," doesn't work, because we live in community. The way that we choose to treat each other individually is called manners, the way that we choose to treat each other in large groups is called politics. Because faith has so much to do with how we choose to treat each other, our faith of course will influence our political choices in some ways.

– When you read the instruction to "fear God," remember how Martin Luther used that phrase when he wrote the Small Catechism section on the 10 Commandments. Words can have many meanings, and when we talk about "fearing" God we mean having respect for God's incredible power.

Slavery & the Bible – Philemon 8-21

Before beginning this Bible study, take a look at the What's The Story section at the beginning of Philemon in your AF Lutheran Study Bible and choose what information about the book to share with your students.

-v. 8-10 – The author is calling himself Onesimus' (*ohn-nee-see-mus*) father, specifically his father in the faith. When someone says they are another person's "parent in the faith," what do you think that means? Do we have something like that today? (*Baptismal sponsors, confirmation mentors. Not so much pastors, they often move around, it's a different relationship.*)

-**v. 11-14** – The author wants a good deed, what, we don't know yet, to be by choice and not forced- this might remind you of our Bible study when we learned about the Reformation.

-**v. 15-16** – Here we find out what the good deed is- Onesimus was the slave of the person being written to, and now that they are siblings in Christ, the author is hoping that the slave-owner will voluntarily choose to free Onesimus. Slavery is always wrong, but in Biblical times when certain kinds of slavery were common, it was still especially evil to enslave a sibling.

-**v. 17-21** – Here the author declares himself and Onesimus absolutely equal. Paul, born free, an educated man of respectability in the Jewish world, a learned artisan (he made tents, and it took a lot of skill to make tents that could stand up to desert storms) was equal to a slave! What an extraordinary statement for him to have made. What does this passage tell us about Christianity and slavery?

ELCA History – Romans 14:13-23

-**v. 13-16** – (*This passage also calls back to the dream about the unclean animals "in a sheet" in Acts 10, referencing that may be helpful.*) Do these verses say that we, as modern Christians, have to follow Jewish food laws? (*No, we don't, because nothing is clean or unclean in itself.*) What about Christians back in Jesus' day who were born Jewish? (*They might choose to but wouldn't have to. Most Christians at the start of the church considered themselves a subset of Judaism, rather than separate from it. If they chose to follow the laws it would be because they were honoring their heritage, not because they felt required to. In the same way today, if a Jewish person converted to Christianity they might choose to continue following those laws. However, because there is a lot of very ugly church history about how the church has treated the Jewish people over the centuries, we don't make an effort to convert Jewish people to Christianity* *now. If they come of their own free will, that's fine, but we don't go out of our way.)*

-v. 17-21 – In short, this passage tells us to not let things that aren't hurting anyone, hurt the church. On the whole that's a good idea, we even have a word for it, adiaphora (*ah-dee-ah-for-ah*), things that might matter to some of us but aren't important enough to cause a serious argument in the church. But historically, this passage has been used to argue against things like the abolition of slavery, and the start of ordaining women as pastors. The difference is, that did hurt people, and therefore also hurt the church, as opposed to not eating meat when dining with people who are vegetarians for religious reasons, or not drinking wine when with people who are teetotalers for religious reasons- that doesn't hurt you at all.

-v. 22-23 – We might believe or practice our faith a little differently than our fellow siblings in Christ, but that doesn't mean we aren't still Christians together. Allowing people to be, say, superstitious, as long as they're not hurting anyone or anything by it is one thing- it allows them to not hurt themselves. But if people are getting hurt, then it's time to take action.

ELCA Structure & Ministries – 1 Timothy 3:1-13

Before starting this Bible study, take a look at the Background File at the start of 1 Timothy to discover who wrote this book. Also, read the last paragraph of the What's the Story, to learn who the author is writing the letter to.

-v. 1-2- These verses list positive characteristics a bishop or church leader should have, but translating from the original language isn't always simple. See note A at the bottom of p. 1955 to learn how a small change in translation can change the meaning of a phrase.

-v. 3-5- Continuing, verse 3 lists characteristics a bishop/church leader shouldn't have. The next 2 verses put certain demands on their family. Are having these rules for a church leader's family a good idea in today's world? (*It's unlikely the family had a say in the leader's choice of career. And what if the church leader is being unjust? Also, adding extra stress to a family of a person in a high-stress job isn't likely to help.*)

-v. 6-7- What does the author mean by verse 6- what dangers could having too much pride have for a church leader? Is verse 7 still true today, does the way a leader appear to those outside a church community matter?

-v. 8-10- Do you know what the term deacon means in the ELCA? What does it mean to say they shouldn't be "double-tongued"? If you're not sure what the "mystery of faith" is, look at the margin note for verse 9 and skip ahead to verse 16 to learn more.

-v. 11-13- What does it mean to be a slanderer? To be temperate? Are these requirements only for women?

Career Ministry – 1 Corinthians 12:1-13

Read the margin note at the start of chapter 12 to begin.

-v. 1-3- Verse 2 illustrates one reason why the 1st Commandment is important. According to verse 3, does it sound like faith is some-thing we do independently & entirely on our own? (*When we speak it's by the Holy Spirit.*)

-v. 4-7- What does the word manifestation mean? So what is a spiritual gift according to this passage? (*The Holy Spirit becoming alive and real and working among us.*)

-v. 8-11- This passage lists some spiritual gifts, but not all of them, can you think of any others? (*helpfulness, music, peacemakers, being kind in spite of difficulty*)

-**v. 12-13**- Are some of these gifts "more important" than others to God? See margin note. Are some more important to us? Should they be?

Other Lutheran Denominations – Galatians 3:23-4:7

-**v. 23-24**- What law were we under before faith came? (*the holiness code in the Hebrew Scriptures*) When these verses say, "before faith came" they're talking about a historical event than happened, can you guess what it is? (*Jesus!*)

-**v. 25-27**- So who is a child of God? (*all Christians*) What about people who have been baptized in other Christian faith traditions like Catholics & Orthodox? (*them too*)

-**v. 28-29**- See the margin note for v. 27-29. What do these verses mean for how we treat people- of different nationalities, richer or poorer than us, or of another gender than us? What do these verses mean for how the church should treat people?

-**v. 1-3**- What does the word "minor" mean here? (*someone who's not an adult yet*) So if a minor inherits lots of money from a will, do they control it right away? The reference to "elemental spirits" is further explained in the margin note for v. 8-10. Can celebrating a holiday or festival, even if it's a religious one, become more important to us than the faith behind it?

-**v. 4-7**- God sent the Spirit into our hearts? When does that happen? (*baptism!*)

Other Christian Denominations – 1 Corinthians 12:12-26

Before you begin, read the margin note for v. 12-30.

-**v. 12-13**- When we say there's only one baptism, we don't just mean in the Lutheran church, but in the whole Christian church. When this passage talks about "the body" it's helpful to remember that just after this passage ends, Paul makes it clear that he's talking about the body of Christ- the church.

-**v. 14-20**- The church is one body, but the members of the body have many gifts. Who in the church helps the body of Christ to "see"? To "hear"? In v. 19 Paul implies that if we all had the same gift instead of variety, we'd be a giant eyeball or a giant nose, instead of a body. What good would that be?

-**v. 21-26**- In v. 23 Paul points out that there are some parts of the body that we generally always keep clothed, which we think of as being less respectable, but by putting all that time & effort into clothing them, we're showing them honor, which is good because we really can't do without them. In the same way, there may be members of the church who the world would tell us are "less respectable" but we know that we can't do without them either, and therefore we treat them with more respect and honor.

Other Religions – Luke 10:25-37

The fill in the blank answer for the discussion question related to Islam, is the KKK. This can lead to further conversation about how, just like Christians don't want the KKK associated with them, Muslims around the world don't want extremists associated with them, either.

-**v. 25-28**- The lawyer's answer to Jesus' question are also, elsewhere in the Bible, called the two greatest commandments, and the "sum of the law"- the total meaning of the law.

-**v. 29-32**- We have priests today, but we don't use the word Levite very often, do you know who a Levite was? (*belongs to the tribe of Israel responsible for the care & upkeep of the Temple and the group the priests are chosen from, so he might not be a priest but would have religious responsibilities and be respected*)

-**v. 33-37**- The Samaritans were a neighboring group who, a long time before Jesus tells this story, had been Jewish, but built their own Temple up north where they lived. The Jewish people further south believed only their Temple could truly be dedicated to God, and declared the Samaritans were no longer Jewish. The two groups continued to clash through Biblical times. There are still Samaritans in that area today, though not very many of them, and they still have their Temple. So given that background, what is this passage saying about people who aren't Christian? Can they be good neighbors? How should we treat them?

Season of Pentecost Holidays – Acts 2:1-14, 22-24, 37-42

Look through the Background File section at the beginning of the book of Acts, especially the first two paragraphs, before you begin this study and summarize this for your students as they open their Bibles.

-**v. 1-4** – Who are the "they" referred to in this passage? Look at the last verse of Acts chapter 1 to find out. (*The remaining disciples, after Jesus' ascension.*) Suddenly there are "tongues of fire" and a big violent wind, WHOOOSH! So loud the people outside could hear it! Does this part remind you of another Bible story? Check out the note on verse 4. (*References Tower of Babel, you may have to retell it a bit.*)

-**v. 5-11** – (*The leader may want to lead this section with the many unfamiliar names.*) Take a look at the map on p. 1797 to see how far these people travelled. (*If possible, compare this to a modern map to show what countries are there today. Pick one of the further away spots that someone travelled to Jerusalem from, and find a place that is the same distance from your classroom to give a sense of scale. Remind the students the options for travel were sailing ship, horseback/wagon, or walking!*)

-**v. 12-14** – Would you react like the crowd did at all this? At this point Peter quotes Joel 2:28-32, so we skip down to verse 22.

-**v. 22-24** – This is called the "3 Verse Gospel." Peter then quotes Psalm 16:8-11. By tying everything into the Hebrew Scriptures, Peter is telling the crowd, made up of Jewish people from all over the world, that the long-awaited Messiah has come.

-v. 37-42 – Okay, so 3,000 people were baptized in a day. How many people attend worship each Sunday? So how many services would it take to hold 3,000 people? Can you imagine what that must have looked like, how long it took, what a mess it made of the river? This story is why we call Pentecost the Birthday of the Church, because the church multiplied in size so many times over on that one day, because of one short speech by Peter.

Seasons Related to Christmas -Matthew 2:7-23

-v. 7-12: See note C at the bottom of the page- in this time and place it was taken for granted that the stars and their movements had supernatural meanings. Astrologers were the people who closely studied the stars, there were no purely scientific astronomers at this point, as far as we know. So that would explain why Herod called for these people to ask about a star. How many wise men are there, according to Matthew? (*doesn't say, not just 3*) Gold, frankincense & myrrh are all very valuable, easy to transport items, which would be helpful to have for trade when making the long journey in the next verses.

-v. 13-18: Even as a toddler, Jesus is seen as a threat to those in power. Are Herod's choices in verse 16 part of the prophecy mentioned in v. 15? (*no, Jesus just had to get to Egypt in order to be called from there*) So who would be responsible for the deaths of those children, God, or Herod? (*Herod, who had free will*) However we don't have any historical proof that this event actually happened, historians of the time don't mention it, and it's extraordinary enough that they probably would have. This is probably a story-telling method from the author of Matthew to show us that Jesus was a threat to the powerful from the start, and that the prophecies of the Hebrew Scriptures played a vital role in his life.

-**v. 19-23:** Matthew is the Gospel where we see Joseph being very active when Jesus is a baby, in Luke the focus is more on Mary. See the margin note for v. 22- there are multiple men in the New Testament who go by the name of Herod! This is why we see one when Jesus is a child, and another (Herod Antipas) when he's an adult. The margin note for v. 23 also provides some interesting information on the multiple meanings of "Nazorean."

Seasons Related to Easter – John 20:19-29

-**v. 19-23**- In Biblical Greek, the same word can be translated as "breath" or "spirit"- so what Jesus breathes onto the disciples in v. 22 is the Spirit!

-**v. 24-25**- Does Thomas remind you of anyone in your life in these verses? Is that attitude a bad thing? When was the last time you said, "prove it!," about something?

-**v. 26-29**- What is the difference between doubt, and unbelief?

Priesthood of All Believers – Romans 12:4-14

The Equal in Call discussion question can be a time to remind students that, just because they themselves aren't interested in a certain career, or it doesn't have much prestige, doesn't mean that the people in those jobs can't truly find them a vocation. Especially jobs that involve serving the community and helping others.

-**v. 4-8** – What does the word prophecy mean? Exhortation? (*In the Bible prophets understood and explained God's will, also sometimes includes telling the future, which is the common meaning now. To exhort is somewhere between encouraging someone and ordering them to do something, there's enthusiasm involved but it isn't subservient, it's not begging. There's an expectation that the thing you're encouraging them to do is good and righteous.*)

– There's a list of gifts different people have here, can you think of other gifts people use in the church or to do God's work in the world? (*Try to steer away from being good at school and towards gifts like kindness, being a good listener, doing the tasks nobody else wants to do without complaining.*)

– Are any of these gifts more important than the others? (*Various answers.*) Are any of them holier than the others? (*No.*)

-v. 9-14 – What does "let love be genuine" mean here? (*Various examples of faked or abusive "love."*) Why is love being genuine important for Christians?

– What does "outdo one another in showing honor" actually look like in your daily life? How about "bless those that persecute you"?

Spiritual Disciplines -Acts 2:42-47

This passage happens just after the Day of Pentecost, the "birthday of the church," when 3,000 people were baptized in one day not long after Jesus ascended.

-v. 42 – Teaching, fellowship, breaking bread, & prayers: what does this sound like to you? (*Worship!*)

-v. 43-45 – What would this be like? Have you ever heard of this before? See the margin note on these verses. (*Various religious orders, charities, & communism may come up.*)

-v. 46-47 – (*See the alternate word choices listed for these verses.*) "Having the goodwill of all the people," who are "all the people"? Does this include those who aren't part of the church? (*Sounds like it!*) What does this whole passage say about how we should treat non-Christians? About how we should do evangelism? (*We shouldn't be mean or condescending to non-Christians, evangelism needs to include respect for those we talk to, and we still need Christian fellowship & support while doing evangelism. Group worship matters!*)

– What spiritual practices do you see in these verses? (*Worship, communion, stewardship, charity, evangelism, etc.*)

Stewardship – Deuteronomy 26:1-11

-**v. 1-5a (*end at start of quotation*)** – Here we're talking about agricultural first fruits, crops. Why would giving first fruits, rather than last, be important here? (*You can choose to give the best rather than what's left over, nothing will have spoiled yet, you won't run out before you give to God.*)

–We might not own land or plant crops. What has God given you? (*Don't forget gifts that aren't things you can touch! Ultimately the answer is, everything, but take your time getting there, to get a good variety of responses.*) If you rephrased that first statement the person making the offering makes in v. 4, for yourself, what would you say? (*Putting your gift that you can give "first fruits" of in place of land.*)

-**v. 5b-10a (*end at end of quotation*)** – See the margin note about the Aramean. God also renamed Jacob, Israel, which is the name the Jewish people took after he died.

– Reread the last sentence of this quotation. Why is this person making an offering? (*Because really it belongs to God anyway. Hint: that's also true for us.*)

-**v. 10b-11** – What happens to the offering in the Bible passage? (*Levites are priests.*) What happens to the offering that you give at church? (*Spend awhile talking about the many places that money goes.*)

Worship Whys -Revelation 2-3

(*Instead of going through these by verses, give each student or pair of students one of the letters to read through. Thyatira is a little more complicated than the others, a leader could do that one as an example.*) What is that congregation's greatest strength? Greatest weakness? Are those strengths and weaknesses still present in the church today? (*Not every congregation will have both a strength and a weakness listed.*)

Special Services – Ruth 1:6-18

Naomi and her husband were Israelites who had moved to Moab, a neighboring country, years before and raised two sons to adulthood there. Their sons married Ruth and Orpah. Then Naomi's husband and both of her sons died, Ruth and Orpah not having borne children yet. That's where our passage starts.

-v. 6-10 – What do we know about Naomi's relationship with her daughters-in-law? (*She cares for them.*)

– Why did Naomi tell them to leave her? (*To return to their families so they could remarry. Remarrying would be much easier for them in a land where they are not strangers.*)

– What does Naomi wish for Ruth & Orpah? (*That God will be as kind to them as they were to their dead husbands and to Naomi, and that they may remarry to have a safe future.*)

-v. 11-14 – Traditionally in Israel, a widow who had not had children, which were basically her retirement plan, had the option to marry one of her husband's brothers, who she could have a child with, and that child would be legally considered the heir of her first husband, and care for her in her old age. Why doesn't that work for Ruth & Orpah here? (*Naomi's children are all dead and she is too old to bear another.*)

–Was Orpah's choice to return to her family a bad choice? Is she a bad person? (*No.*)

-v.15-18 – Do Ruth's promises sound familiar? (*Wedding vows!*) Can you see elements in these verses that remind you of a funeral and a healing service as well? (*The reference to death & burial is pretty obvious. Also here Ruth chooses her community, Naomi, and offers her support to Naomi, which also happens during a healing service.*)

– Ruth says she will worship God because Naomi will. Is that how faith works today? (*These days faith doesn't entirely depend on who your family is. Understanding the historical context that your faith was almost always defined by your family in Biblical times and for centuries after, is helpful to understand many Bible stories- like Lydia's household being baptized with her, and the amazement that early Christians would leave the faith of their families for Christianity.*)

Lutherans & the Bible – Acts 8:26-40

The question for the final section of this lesson involves the old rumor of "the Shakespeare Psalm." The idea is that either Shakespeare was involved with the King James Version's translation and left his name in this Psalm as a "calling card," or the King arranged for it as a tribute to him. No historical document proves these theories, but Shakespeare would have been 46 years old in 1611, when the translation was published.

-**v. 26-29** – Philip is an early Christian. The Ethiopian (*the ancient church called him Simeon if you want to name him*) being a "eunuch" (*pronounced "you-nuhk"*) means that he is a slave, not a free person, who has had his choice of whether to have biological children taken away from him- he never can now.

-**v. 30-35** – Philip tells the Ethiopian that this passage from Isaiah is about who? (*Jesus!*) Why would this passage from Isaiah be powerful for the Ethiopian in particular? (*Jesus was hurt, humiliated, and treated unjustly. So was the Ethiopian, as a eunuch.*)

-**v. 36-40** – Please read v. 37 out loud again? (*What, it's not there?!*) There was a verse here in many older English translations, including the KJV. However since the 1600s when that was translated, we've found many older copies of the Biblical texts than we had in the 1600s. Sometimes, a verse here and there was found in the newer copies, but not in the oldest versions (*emphasis on there being multiple older versions*) we had access to. This lead translators to believe these verses only found in the newer copies of the texts were added by people along the way, so these verses often aren't included in modern translations, and only appear in footnotes.

– Which of the 3 ways the Word of God comes to us did the Ethiopian encounter in this passage? (*Review three ways: Jesus, Holy Spirit, Bible. Ethiopian receives the Word of God through the Holy Spirit both through Philip's teaching and through baptism, is united with Jesus in baptism, and reads Scripture, so all three!*)

The End of All Things – Revelation 20:11-21:8

Before starting this Bible study, take a look at the "What's the Message" section for Revelation in the AF Lutheran Study Bible, and decide what useful highlights from that to share with the students.

-**v. 11-15** – There are two sets of books- those that record the things people did, and "the book of life." What do you think this means? (*What you do is not who you are to God, your life with God is not only about what you do – as discussed elsewhere, good works come naturally through living your faith but they don't "earn" you anything.*)

– Revelation 13:8 & 17:8 say that the names in the "book of life" have been recorded there "from the foundation of the world". The first also says the book of life is the book of the lamb who was slaughtered- Jesus Christ. So if the names there have always been there, what does that say about God's grace? (*That the grace of God is sure and certain- don't forget we haven't gotten to exactly whose names are written there yet.*)

– In v. 14 it says Death & Hades are thrown into the lake of fire. So the event of death, and the place where the dead lived according to who the author of Revelation was writing to, the Greeks, were destroyed. So this verse says death, the event and the place of it, are gone and no more.

– What is this "lake of fire"? It's a reference to something Jesus talked about in his Sermon on the Mount. Jesus didn't talk about the afterlife a lot but he did mention a place called "Gehenna," in that passage. Gehenna was a real place in Jesus' time, it was an area just outside the city of Jerusalem, a valley that was used as a trash dump. By Jesus' time it had been a trash dump literally for generations, and in an effort to reduce the amount of trash in it so more trash could be dumped in, it had been lit on fire, only there was so much trash and new trash was being put in so often than it was basically always on fire somewhere, therefore it was called a "lake of fire." Keep in mind rain doesn't happen often in a desert so the fire didn't really go out. Jesus always talks about Gehenna firmly as a metaphor, not as a literal description of the afterlife. Usually when the Bible talks about fire as a metaphor, it's purifying things, burning away flaws, sins, or in the case of one of Jesus' parables, the chaff of wheat.

-v. 1-4 – What would a new version of our community look like? What would be different? What would be the same? (*Answers will vary. Don't forget how the people will change.*) What about the lack of death? What would that change? (*Again, imagination is good here. Imagine the culture clash of very different generations! Yet we are all God's beloved children.*)

-v. 5-8 – Is this a complete new start that God's doing here, or is this God changing what already exists? Notice that going to the second death of the lake of fire is a list of characteristics (*see 9:21*) all of which are versions of idolatry, putting something else before the importance of God in one's life. What would purifying these mean? (*Like the chaff in Jesus' parable, perhaps.*)

-Go back to v. 6, when God says, "I am the Alpha and the Omega, the beginning and the end." So what does God mean by "I am the beginning"? (*Everything ever created was created by God, God was before everything else.*) So if that's what being the beginning is, what does it mean that God is the end? Does God continue longer than the lake of fire, the second death, the various metaphors & images in Revelation? Does God ever end? (*Yes, God exists longer than any of those; no, God does not end.*) Does that mean this passage ends on a note of hope, or despair? (*As long as God is, God's grace is, we cannot despair in the face of God's relentless grace.*)

Spiritual Self Defense – Ezekiel 34:1-6

The author here is confronting how unfaithful the people of Israel have been, especially their irresponsible leaders, or "shepherds," as they live in exile.

-**v. 1-2a** – (*Stop just before the author starts quoting the Lord.*) Who is the "me" in this part- who is speaking? Who is this passage directed at? (*The author, who is speaking to the leaders of Israel.*)

-**v. 2b-3** – What have the "shepherds" done? What have they left undone? (*They have been feeding themselves instead of their people, they have been getting rich rather than taking care of their people.*)

-**v. 4** – What do each of these undone tasks look like today? (*Various examples- as many that we can do as possible.*)

-**v. 5-6** – We aren't actually talking about sheep here, are we? (*No, we're talking about the people who the leaders should have been taking care of.*) So if the sheep are the Israelites, who do they belong to? Sheep don't always belong to the shepherd, who's sheep are they? (*God's sheep, and so are we!*)

-

-

Oppression in the Bible – Matthew 15:21-28

-v. 21-22 – (*Make sure everyone can pronounce Canaanite [cain-nahn-ite] and knows this person is not an Israelite, one of Jesus' own people, but an inhabitant of this foreign land Jesus is travelling in.*) Jesus and the disciples had to walk through Samaria to get to where they are in this story, it was a long journey north, so they aren't here accidentally. The woman who approaches Jesus says her daughter has been possessed by a demon, does anyone have any ideas for what that might mean with today's medical knowledge? (*She probably had a mental illness, or may have been having seizures, or narcolepsy- unexplained behavior that wasn't recognized as a common illness.*)

-v. 23-25 – Why do the disciples want her to leave? (*Her shouting is bothering them.*) Jesus isn't really talking about sheep here, who does he say he's been sent to? (*The people of Israel, the Jewish people, who he was born into, and who are lost, occupied by the Roman military.*) Who sent Jesus? (*God. Just checking!*)

-v. 26-28 – Jesus just insulted her! What do you think about this? (*Being horrified is okay, the truth is we don't know exactly why Jesus said this, or why the person who wrote this Gospel decided to record it. However, Jesus just choosing to speak to this woman at all, broke several rules- she's a woman, she's not related to him, she's not Jewish, he's not in "teaching mode" but instead travelling. If someone suggests Jesus used the word for "puppy" and may have meant it in a fond way, point out this is a grown woman with a child in danger, and ask if their mom, in the same situation, would appreciate being called a puppy.*)

– Why does Jesus decide to heal her daughter? (*She showed her faith by insisting she had a right to be helped. She did so in a subservient way- she had probably heard the disciples complaining about her and ap-*

proaching a crowd of strange men as a woman alone could have been scary- but she stood up to him.)

– What does this story tell us about who Jesus, and the Gospel, is sent to now? (*Everyone! Including foreigners, those who aren't "respectable," those who are scared, those who receive the Gospel not by their own action but because someone else reached out for it on their behalf- the little girl did nothing to be healed, and more!)*

Science & Faith – Job 38:4-21

Go through these verses slowly and talk about the scientific advances since ancient times that are related to each one of God's statements and questions. Many experts believe Job may be the first book of the Bible to ever be written down, even before Genesis was, so this goes back long before Jesus' time.

A few to get you started: v. 5 is related to mapmaking- we've gotten so much better at this over the years, even just the last thirty years with advances in GPS technology. V. 6 relates to geology- we know a lot now about how different kinds of rocks are formed, under what conditions, how long it takes, even carbon dating is related to this. V. 7 reminds us of the very long way that astronomy has come, etc.

In the end, all these scientific advancements have taught us that the universe is far more complicated than our long-ago ancestors ever imagined. But we also know that it's not like the universe used to be simple and is complicated now, all these forces and mechanisms and processes were always going on, interacting with each other to bring about new things. All this comes from God, this is the marvelous Creation that God has made! As often as we give thanks for Creation we rarely explore the scope of it, from tiniest atom to unimaginably enormous galaxies spread over unfathomable space.

Appendix: How to Use This Book

Are you hoping to learn more about Christianity & the Lutheran approach to faith on your own? Wonderful! I hope this book may be helpful to you. While it was originally designed for teaching middle and high schoolers, I hope I've managed to arrange it so it's helpful for anyone, age 12 to 112. You'll want a Bible (I suggest the Lutheran Study Bible from Augsburg Fortress) and maybe a copy of Martin Luther's Small Catechism to use with this book.

Want to know what makes being Lutheran special? How to practice your faith more intentionally every day? What all Christians have in common, and what we've been disagreeing about for 2,000 years? Why the worship service is arranged like it is? What's up with funerals and what happens after we die? What's a Trinity, anyway?

I hope this book will help with all those questions and more. But while this can be useful start, let me say that there is one thing vital to any Christian, young or old, brand new or cradle baptized: a faith community. Please find a group of fellow Christians you can worship with, who will support you in your life and faith journey. Because there's one question I bet you're asking: Why did God put us here? And the answer, as far as I can tell, is simple: each other.

Are you a Confirmation student? Excellent! Look, I realize you may not have a lot of choice in attending these classes- but I bet the same is true for when you learn things like math and history too, right? Well just like both of those are going to help you in your life, both now and as a grown up (because how else will you manage your money and figure out who to vote for?), this program is designed to help you figure out what being an adult Christian really looks like. I put this program together because I have two nightmares when it comes to Confirmation, and far too many programs out there fulfill one or both.

The first nightmare is a Confirmation program that treats you like a small child. The whole point of Confirmation is that you're becoming an adult! You're not quite one yet, but that doesn't mean you should be treated like a 7-year-old. The questions you'll be asked to consider in this book will take some thought, they aren't just "memorize an answer and spit it out" questions. You'll be thinking about your life now, when you were younger, and your hopes and dreams for when you get older. And yes, there's actual content in these lessons: you're getting to an age where you can understand that the world is more complex than you thought it was when you were 7, and addressing that takes some time.

The second nightmare I have is a Confirmation program that doesn't seem to have anything to do with how you live your actual life. Learning about your faith doesn't make much of a difference if it doesn't follow you from Sunday morning to Saturday night. Pretty much all the questions you'll be asked in this book are directly to do with your everyday life. The smallest decisions you make each day are affected by your faith, and this book explores just how that works.

One more thing I want you to remember: attending the classes may not be your choice, but going through with the actual Confirmation ceremony is ***always, entirely, absolutely your choice.*** No one wants you to stand up in front of literally God and everybody and lie in church. If you come to your last year of Confirmation and you're not sure you can say those words and mean them, please, talk to someone. Your parents, teacher, pastor, baptismal sponsor- any adult you trust. Maybe you'd like to take another year to consider it first. Maybe you still have questions that haven't been answered. Maybe you've had a really emotional year and you're just not up for another milestone. Or maybe you're not sure you want to be part of the church at all. It's okay – serious decisions are a part of adult life, and that includes life in the church. Down the road, when you're ready, the church will still be here, and ready to welcome you.

Are you teaching a Confirmation class? Congratulations! This is one of the most exciting parts of ministry, I'm so glad you decided to take part in it. When you look at your class, just think: you never know who they'll grow up to be. The love and attention you show them is going to have a big impact on who they become. Take a deep breath, and don't forget to bring the Holy Spirit with you to class!

A few quick notes. This program is meant for small classes or small group discussion – the discussion is vital! No tech is required in class (unless someone's using an ebook version on their smart phone), all your students need is this book, a copy of the Small Catechism, and their Lutheran Study Bible from Augsburg Fortress. A few questions (not too many) do assume the students have internet access somewhere in their lives, if necessary you may need to work around that. Each lesson has a Bible passage and a hymn with it. Outlines for Bible study with the class are in the appendix, to adjust as needed. Some are longer and detailed, and others are shorter and more straightforward. The hymns are chosen by theme but also are the more popular hymns that are likely to have big words or poetic imagery, which the students may not have considered or understood before.

When I first developed this program, I set it up to have the students read the lesson ahead of class each week, so they could think about the questions and write down any further questions they had. Then in class we very briefly discussed each section, and then discussed the questions more deeply, and at the end we did the Bible study, which generally took about a third of the class time. (I really do suggest looking at the Bible passages **after** you finish with the lesson, they were chosen to expand on themes you'll already have talked about.) Then if there's time, we read the verses of the hymn aloud, and maybe listened to a recording of the music, making sure everyone understood what the words meant. Each session ended with us going around the table sharing one thing we'd be praying about during the coming week and praying together. There's space at the end of each lesson for the students to write down what they'll pray about. Eventually I added two rules to this: no praying for certain kinds of weather; and if prayers involved sports in some way, to pray only that the players are not injured and show good sportsmanship, and not for a certain team to win. You may not need to institute those.

Another helpful part of the program was to have each student choose a Confirmation mentor –a confirmed or adult member of the congregation, who were not the student's parent or sibling. The mentor was welcome to attend classes (few could regularly, but the variety helped our conversations a lot) and helped the student with their projects and questions. This gives the student another positive adult presence in their life, and always having more than one adult in the room was great for keeping the conversation going (though it sometimes helped drag us further off topic...). Letting the students choose their own mentor turned out to be the real secret to the whole thing: only the student really knows who'll they'll be comfortable with, and the adults loved being asked by the students.

When I say, don't forget to bring the Holy Spirit with you to class? The Spirit's going to show up anyway. The unexpected will happen. Some days you'll feel blessed, others... less so. That's life. Don't be afraid to say, "I don't know, I'll have to pray about that." Or, "That's interesting, can you tell me more about that?" Or, "I was wrong, I'm sorry." Your students, their mentors, and the Holy Spirit are all going to combine to surprise and amaze you. You may feel like your own faith has been turned upside down and had its pockets shaken out for loose change. That's good! It means you care.

Whatever reason you're reading this book, I hope it brings you grace, peace, joy, and above all – more questions! May God's love surround you and protect you every day of your life.

Acknowledgments

For their unceasing support and excitement about this project, which has kept me going, I have far too many colleagues to name. But I'd especially thank those in Young Clergy Women International, the ELCA Clergy Facebook Group, and the ELCA 2030 Rostered Leaders Facebook Group.

I could not have done this without the vital help of those who know better than I on any number of topics. Especially I'd like to thank my old friend Father Marcus Knecht, my cousin Angela Ibsen, and my colleague Rev. Brian McClinton for their assistance in making this project possible.

I've had many cheerleaders and many who have walked with me in the past few years, but above all my husband, Rory, has been my pillar of strength. Thank you so much, love.

Works Cited

Arand, Charles P, and Robert Kolb. *The Book of Concord: The Confessions of the Evangelical Lutheran Church.* Minneapolis Fortress Press, 2005.

Dietrich Bonhoeffer. *The Cost of Discipleship.* London: Scm Press, 2015.

Evangelical Lutheran Church in America. *Human Sexuality: Gift and Trust*, 2009. Accessed May 28, 2020. https://download.elca.org/ELCA%20Resource%20Repository/SexualitySS.pdf.

———. *The Use of the Means of Grace: A Statement on the Practice of Word and Sacrament.* Minneapolis, Mn: Augsburg Fortress, 1997.

Evangelical Lutheran Church Of Canada, and Evangelical Lutheran Church in America. *Evangelical Lutheran Worship.* Minneapolis: Augsburg Fortress, 2006.

Gerlach, Wolfgang, and Victoria Barnett. *And the Witnesses Were Silent: The Confessing Church and the Persecution of the Jews.* Lincoln: University Of Nebraska Press, 2000.

Wiesel, Elie. "One Must Not Forget." Interview by Alvin P. Sanoff. *US News & World Report*, October 27, 1986.

"Athanasian Creed." Christian Reformed Church in North America, 1987. Last modified 1987. Accessed May 28, 2020. https://www.crcna.org/welcome/beliefs/creeds/athanasian-creed.

The Holy Bible: Containing the Old and New Testaments: New Revised Standard Version. Grand Rapids: Zondervan, 1989.

Images

AnonMoos. *Compact Version of a Basic Minimal (Equilateral Triangular) Version of the "Shield of the Trinity" or "Scutum Fidei" Diagram of Traditional Christian Symbolism, with Original Latin Captions. Wikimedia,* November 18, 2009. Accessed May 28, 2020. commons.wikimedia.org.

AnonMoos, and Melian. *Jerusalem Cross Symbol of Traditional Heraldry - Variant with Large Cross Potent (Instead of Large Greek Cross). Wikimedia,* October 8, 2005. Accessed May 28, 2020. commons.wikimedia.org.

Boris23. *Basic Latin Cross. Wikimedia,* January 27, 2006. Accessed May 28, 2020. commons.wikimedia.org.

OpenClipArt. *A Vector Silhouette Drawing of Jesus Christ on the Cross. Black and White Illustration of Crucifixion. FreeSVG,* January 22, 2014. Accessed May 28, 2020. https://freesvg.org/christ-on-the-cross-vector-image.

Rohloff, Katherine. *Simple Depiction of Maslow's Hierarchy of Needs,* 2020.

Vodicka, Petr. *Celtic Cross, Created with Sodipodi Vector Software. Ornamental Version of Celtic "High Cross" with Decorative Knotwork by Petr Vodicka. Wikimedia,* n.d. Accessed May 28, 2020. commons.wikimedia.org.

Another Celtic Cross. Also USVA Headstone Emblem 46. Wikimedia, March 25, 2012. Accessed May 28, 2020. commons.wikimedia.org.

Rev. Katherine Rohloff is an ELCA pastor and a "Double Burger", having graduated from Wartburg College and Wartburg Theological Seminary. She's enjoyed producing HP@Church, a podcast relating scripture with themes from the Harry Potter series, with her colleague Rev. Emily Elizabeth Ewing. She and her family live in southern Minnesota.